YOU CAN

Be a Successful SCHOOL LEADER

Anthony David

FOR AGES 4-11

"Effective leadership is vital, if we are to achieve a world-class education system..."
Lord Andrew Adonis, 2007

Acknowledgements

Author
Anthony David

Editor
Nicola Morgan

Development Editor
Kate Pedlar

Project Editor
Fabia Lewis

Series Designer
Catherine Perera

Cover Designer
Anna Oliwa/Catherine Perera

Cover photography
© Ingram Publishing

Design
Q2A Media

Text © 2009, Anthony David
© 2009 Scholastic Ltd

Designed using Adobe InDesign

Published by Scholastic Ltd
Villiers House
Clarendon Avenue
Leamington Spa
Warwickshire CV32 5PR

www.scholastic.co.uk

Printed by Bell and Bain Ltd.
1 2 3 4 5 6 7 8 9   9 0 1 2 3 4 5 6 7 8

Mixed Sources
Product group from well-managed forests and other controlled sources
www.fsc.org Cert no. TT-COC-002769
© 1996 Forest Stewardship Council

Anthony David dedicates this book to his father.

© Crown copyright and other materials reproduced under the terms of the Click Use Licence. Extracts from The Bichard Inquiry Report by Sir Michael Bichard © Parliamentary copyright 2004. National College of School Leadership for use of extracts from *Leading Coaching in Schools* © 2008, NCSL (2008, www.ncsl.org.uk). The Primary Review for use of extracts from The Primary Review © 2008, The Primary Review (2008, Cambridge Faculty of Education, Cambridge University). Professor Tim Brighouse for use of an extract from *How successful headteachers survive and thrive* © 2007, Professor Tim Brighouse (2008, www.rm.com).Training and Development Agency for Schools for the use of an extract from *Developing people who support learning* © 2008, Training and development Agency for Schools (2008, www.tda.gov.uk).

British Library Cataloguing-in-Publication Data
A catalogue record for this book is available from the British Library.
ISBN 978-1407-10196-5

The right of Anthony David to be identified as the author of this work has been asserted by him in accordance with the Copyright, Designs and Patents Act 1988.

All rights reserved. This book is sold subject to the condition that it shall not, by way of trade or otherwise, be lent, hired out or otherwise circulated without the publisher's prior consent in any form of binding or cover other than that in which it is published and without a similar condition, including this condition, being imposed upon the subsequent purchaser.

No part of this publication may be reproduced, stored in a retrieval system, or transmitted, in any form or by any means, electronic, mechanical, photocopying, recording or otherwise, without the prior permission of the publisher. This book remains in copyright, although permission is granted to copy pages where indicated for classroom distribution and use only in the school which has purchased the book, or by the teacher who has purchased the book, and in accordance with the CLA licensing agreement. Photocopying permission is given only for purchasers and not for borrowers of books from any lending service.

Due to the nature of the web, the publisher cannot guarantee the content or links of any of the websites referred to. All links were checked October 2008, but It is the responsibility of the reader to assess the suitability of websites and check that links are still live.

Every effort has been made to trace copyright holders for the works reproduced in this book, and the publishers apologise for any inadvertent omissions.

Contents

Introduction **5**

Chapter 1 You can... Develop leadership qualities .. **6**
You can... Identify leadership characteristics **6**
You can... Define your roles and responsibilities **7**
You can... Be a lead learner **8**
You can... Lead on inclusion **9**
You can... Be a coach **10**
You can... Invest in emotional intelligence **11**
You can... Lead professional development **12**
You can... Plan for staff succession **13**

Chapter 2 You can... Develop a school **14**
You can... Identify the key characteristics of an effective school **14**
You can... Lead an urban school **15**
You can... Lead a small school **16**
You can... Plan a budget **17**
You can... Develop a vision **18**
You can... Complete a robust Self-Evaluation Form **19**
You can... Work with the media **20**
You can... Delegate **21**
You can... Implement a School Improvement Plan **22**
You can... Work with your School Improvement Partner ... **23**
You can... Plan for Ofsted **24**
You can... Empower your community to embrace educational risk **25**
You can... Lead in the future **26**

Chapter 3 You can... Lead learning and teaching ... **27**
You can... Develop your curriculum **27**
You can... Manage behaviour **28**
You can... Ensure quality staff welfare **29**
You can... Observe adults teaching **30**
You can... Lead performance management for all **31**
You can... Track pupil progress **32**

Chapter 4 You can... Work with stakeholders **33**
You can... Have an effective School Leadership Team **33**
You can... Empower middle leaders **34**
You can... Develop teaching assistants **35**
You can... Give your children a voice **36**
You can... Offer extended services at your school **37**
You can... Work with children's centres **38**
You can... Communicate with parents **39**
You can... Report to school governors **40**
You can... Develop international links **41**

Contents

Chapter 5 You can... Manage resources **42**
You can... Manage and develop your site **42**
You can... Manage ICT **43**
You can... Manage subject resources. **44**
You can... Manage a classroom. **45**

Chapter 6 You can... Manage risk **46**
You can... Assess risk. **46**
You can... Recruit **47**
You can... Undertake safeguarding measures **48**
You can... Perform appropriate checks **49**
You can... Resolve complaints. **50**
You can... Understand child protection. **51**
You can... Implement a School Travel Plan **52**

Chapter 7 You can... Get to grips with core documentation **53**
You can... Use books and documentation to support your leadership **53**
You can... Use the internet to support your leadership **54**
You can... Ensure every child matters **55**
You can... Implement the renewed Primary Framework.... **56**
You can... Begin to understand the primary curriculum review and the Primary Review **57**
You can... Apply for Kitemarks **58**

Photocopiables **59**
School self-review and Self-Evaluation Form (SEF) update calendar – autumn term **59**
School self-review and Self-Evaluation Form (SEF) update calendar – spring term **60**
School self-review and Self-Evaluation Form (SEF) update calendar – summer term **61**
School Improvement Plan. **62**

Index **63**

Introduction

Leadership in schools is evolving. Ten years ago it may have been the headteacher who was cautiously referred to as the 'leader'. Now we have School Leadership Teams, middle leaders and class leaders. It has become a complex leadership web. Yet, in truth, teachers are leaders the day they set foot in a classroom and command the attention of 30 individuals. There is little doubt that in the next ten years school leadership is going to evolve rapidly due to opportunities to begin to place the jigsaw pieces of a child's life together in one place. The Children's Plan *(DCSF, 2007),* Every Child Matters *(DfES, 2004), children's centres, revised* National Standards for Headteachers *(DfES, 2004), and the current primary curriculum review are all pointing to a new way of thinking about the needs of the whole child and the whole family.*

Preparing for a brighter future

If we, as leaders, are serious about preparing today's children for a brighter future then we must begin new dialogues with all services and we need to prepare for change. Some of the changes will be practical, with schools opening their doors for far longer periods than in the past, through extended learning or partnerships with children's centres. Some of the changes will be subtle such as new relationships with health professionals, and social services supporting and providing long-needed links with families and carers.

This book offers support and advice on many aspects of change that are currently impacting on school life. It is an exciting time where good leadership can shine from the classroom out into the community. What sort of leaders do we need? What are we looking for in our leaders? If leadership could be distilled into a list of attributes then we would be looking for people with vision, drive, enthusiasm, wisdom, and excellent listening and communication skills. There is no single blueprint for schools and, similarly, there is no single blueprint for leadership. It is born out of experience and personality. The single most important attribute is the ability to communicate and this can only happen when the person knows him or herself and the community with whom they are working.

The last ten years have focused on core subjects and standards. But if experience has taught us anything it is that we have to embrace all services working together. The pieces of the jigsaw are in place but if we want to see the whole picture, we are going to have to look closely at how our schools operate in the future. It is a time for rapid evolution and, where we have seen teaching dramatically change in the last ten years, we are going to see whole school communities changing in the next ten.

You Can... Develop leadership qualities

You Can... Identify leadership characteristics

Leadership is, somewhat surprisingly, a new concept within education. Pre-millennial teachers were managers and the only rightful leader was seen to be the headteacher. Yet the reality is that we all display leadership characteristics from the moment we enter the classroom. The skills needed to be a school leader and a classroom teacher are essentially the same – a passion for your vision, a defined understanding of your own strengths and a desire to grow the potential of those who surround you.

Thinking points

- Warren Bennis, an American scholar widely regarded as the pioneer in the field of leadership studies, differentiated managers from leaders by saying that, 'Managers are people who do things right, while leaders are people who do the right thing.' The step up from a manager to a leader is achieved by people who look at what needs to be done and how to do it.

- Leadership styles are changing within schools. The old model of top-down, headteacher-style leadership is being flattened out to embrace a wider, distributed model of leadership. The advantage of this model is that middle and senior leaders are given genuine powers of responsibility while freeing the headteacher from many day-to-day tasks to concentrate on their core purpose: leading the vision and ethos of the school.

Tips, ideas and activities

School leaders need to develop the following characteristics:

- Be honest – display sincerity and integrity in all your actions. Deceptive behaviour will not inspire trust and is easy to spot.

- Be competent – do what you say you are going to do. Delegate so that what you say can be done will be achieved.

- Understand your vision – effective leaders envision what they want and how to get it.

- Inspire – display confidence in all that you do. Know how to teach and have a full appreciation of the broad educational world. Take charge when necessary but equally show flexibility in your leadership style.

- Be current – keep up to date with current practice and ideas. Attend briefings and read reports.

- Be tolerant – seek out diversity.

- Take risks – have the perseverance to accomplish a goal, regardless of the obstacles. Look confident and calm when under stress.

- Use plain English when speaking or writing documents.

- Be creative – things do not always go to plan but the creative leader will look for an opportunity where there appears to be none. It is your duty to keep morale buoyant and to anticipate change.

You Can... **Develop leadership qualities**

You Can... Define your roles and responsibilities

Modern school leaders must have a lens that focuses outwards as well as inwards if they are to fully appreciate their impact on learning. The National Standards for Headteachers *details clear areas of responsibility for headteachers. The standards were revised in 2004 to include a discrete section on local community, which stated that, 'Headteachers share responsibility for leadership of the wider educational system and should be aware that school improvement and community development are interdependent' (*National Standards for Headteachers, *October 2004). This was a major step beyond the traditional view of the headteacher.*

Thinking points

- A defining aspect of headship is delegation. That said, the role includes jobs that no one else can do including aspects of recruitment, budget setting, child protection and curriculum development. Equally, you will no doubt find yourself undertaking mundane tasks. This is inevitable within an environment of underfunding but don't make it a habitual excuse. You are paid to lead.

- Increasingly, schools are being driven by projects rather than subjects. A School Leadership Team should be aware that their Teaching and Learning Responsibility (TLR) points reflect a level of responsibility rather than a specific specialism and those areas of responsibility should change according to a school's needs.

- It is challenging to motivate oneself at a high level all the time and it is not desirable. Map your time and allow for day-to-day tasks, such as filing, to balance your day. Be in control of your job and not the other way round.

Tips, ideas and activities

- Are you clear about your roles and responsibilities and are your staff and governors clear of theirs? If not, seek advice from the local authority. Your core purpose is to lead and wherever this is eroded it impacts on the whole school. Setting clear roles clarifies expectations and acts as a benchmark.

- Consider the teams with whom you are working. Delegating responsibility for writing action plans, managing the supply budget and leading projects will show your faith in their skills and give colleagues valuable experience of whole-school management.

- You have a responsibility to manage your own professional growth. What professional development have you taken part in over the last year? The National College for School Leadership (NCSL) and the Training and Development Agency for Schools (TDA) have a growing range of training sessions to meet a range of needs.

- Work closely with your local authority or diocese. They will be your primary link to changes within education.

- Be mindful of the Schools Forum and its place within the financial structure of your school. It is often aware of financial changes and so is a useful vehicle for keeping up to date.

- Below are a number of websites to support school leaders:
  - The *National Standards for Headteachers* is available at: http://publications.teachernet.gov.uk
  - For capital investment support, visit www.teachernet.gov.uk (search for 'Role of schools, headteachers and governors').

You Can... **Develop leadership qualities**

You Can... Be a lead learner

School leaders in the UK are often, because of financial constraints, still in the position where they have a teaching responsibility. There is a natural tension between being able to fulfil teaching responsibilities with the duties of a school leader. However, having a teaching responsibility provides you with an ideal opportunity to act as a lead learner for the rest of your staff.

Thinking points

- What have you done about your learning? What books have you read recently (aside from this one, of course)? Do you have a career plan? Your career is, in many ways, linked to your learning. It is worth considering what direction your career has taken over the last five years and where you want to be in five years time. From that you can plan the appropriate learning path you need to make that vision happen.

- A lead learner is an enthusiast for their subject. Your particular specialism may not appeal to all but enthusiasm to learn is infectious.

- Creating an environment of learning empowers people, at all levels, to become 'solution providers' rather than 'problem identifiers'.

Tips, ideas and activities

- Do you have an established culture of learning at all levels? The Training and Development Agency for Schools (TDA), www.tda.gov.uk, can direct you to a comprehensive range of professional development programmes and materials to support learning across a spectrum of levels. Promoting external success such as passing a driving test or learning a language can be celebrated as they demonstrate a commitment by the staff to lifelong learning.

- Celebrate success. Where colleagues have achieved certificates (it may be for First Aid, NQT, NPQH or an unrelated academic success) you may wish to consider presenting their certificate in an assembly. This is a strong message to the children that learning can continue beyond school.

- Your learning needs and those of your staff are as individual as a child's. Have an open door for individual enquiries and professional development.

- As a school leader, one of your responsibilities will be to direct learning. This is not always comfortable if the member of staff is resistant. Your personnel officer or other headteachers within your Network Learning Community ((NLC), see page 42) may be able to offer advice. In these cases, record your actions.

- As a school leader you have a unique view of your learners. Action research can support your understanding of these learners and provide a better learning environment for them.

- Below are some of websites that may support learning in your school:
  - www.ncsl.org.uk (search for the PDF *Leading a research-engaged school*).
  - Use Wikipedia (www.wikipedia.org) to find out about action research.

You Can... **Lead on inclusion**

An inclusive school is one that fully appreciates that every child matters and that their needs should be met by quality-first teaching. It's a big ask. It requires sensitive teaching, rigorous assessment and clear objectives. A school that leads through inclusion is one that is analytical and reflective. It is an evolving process of adaptation where the central goal is to include everyone.

Thinking points

- SureStart (2005) identified three waves of inclusion: wave one is characterised by quality-first teaching for all; wave two introduces additional interventions to enable children to work at age-related expectations or above; and wave three considers highly personalised learning packages for individual learners.

- How are you planning your provision? Effective provision requires considered planning which, in turn, requires appropriate training for a shared understanding of what it is you are trying to achieve. Should it form part of the School Improvement Plan?

Tips, ideas and activities

- Four different aspects need to be evaluated when considering what provision can be made available to your learners: audit of need, comparison with existing provision, evidence of what works, and planning in the light of the available school budget. This interlinked jigsaw will help you to identify what skills you have available to meet individual need. Of these four areas, 'audit of need', is the most sensitive. Needs can be identified through assessments such as, Common Assessment Framework (CAF) referrals or the through the involvement of health/social services or other outside support agencies. A child's needs can change rapidly and a school must be ready to support them as best they can.

- Once you have identified need, consider what professional development might be required to support colleagues. Pupil referral units and local professional development centres should be able to direct you towards appropriate training.

- Identify and ring-fence funding streams, such as Excellence in Cities, EMAG, SEN and wave two intervention, to help manage funding. You should be able to do this by creating a new financial line in the expenditure section of the budget.

- RAISEonline and other electronic-tracking tools can help you to identify quickly where additional provision is required.

- Although all schools are required to adhere to the Disabilities Act (2005) it is not until a child with a disability enters your care that this becomes a sharp reality. Is your school prepared? Are rooms acoustically sound for the hearing impaired? Are fire marshals trained in how to use emergency wheelchairs? These are questions to be asked before a child starts to ensure a positive school experience.

You Can... Develop leadership qualities

You Can... **Be a coach**

Schools are well-grounded in how to mentor colleagues. It is something that comes easily to teachers as it is a natural extension of our skills. Coaching, on the other hand, is subtly different to mentoring. Rather than being the font of all knowledge, a coach aims to promote self-learning where their colleague develops independence as their confidence in decision-making grows.

Thinking points

- The coach's message should be, 'I believe in you, I'm investing in you and I expect your best efforts.' As a result, people sense that the leader cares so they feel motivated to uphold their own high standards of performance and they feel accountable for how well they do.

- A coach allows colleagues time to reflect on their practice, unlike a mentor who works alongside a colleague suggesting how to modify their practice. It is supported, self-driven change through reflection.

- There are many 'how to coach' models but in essence it is supporting your colleague to unpick an issue and identify a solution themselves rather than one being presented to them authoritatively. This should ultimately lead to greater independence of shared leadership.

Tips, ideas and activities

- Establish ground rules. Your colleague should be aware of the difference between coaching and mentoring – you are there to support your colleague in becoming a stronger, independent leader.

- The National College for School Leadership (NCSL) document *Leading coaching in schools* (2005) states that good practice is built upon four essential qualities that both the coach and colleague should share:
    - A desire to make a difference to student learning.
    - A commitment to professional learning.
    - A belief in the abilities of colleagues.
    - A commitment to developing emotional intelligence.

- In order to cultivate this shared understanding, a coach should be grounded in a number of key skills:
    - Establishing trust and a working relationship.
    - Listening.
    - Reflective questioning and probing.
    - Summarising or reflecting on information.
    - Taking prompt action.
    - Reinforcing colleagues' skills and success.
    - Reinforcing confidence by highlighting success.

- Locate a calm place for your meetings. If it is not possible to hold them in school, or if you feel that you will be disturbed, meet off-site such as in a hotel or a café. As a rule of thumb allow 80 per cent of the talk time for your colleague and 20 per cent for you to set the scene, summarise, probe and discuss. Set a diary date for the next meeting so that progress can be monitored.

- Celebrate success and achievements. This can be done by writing a letter to a colleague, which is more personal than an email, or praising a colleague's success within the wider school body.

You Can... Develop leadership qualities

You Can... Invest in emotional intelligence

Daniel Goleman has been the champion for emotional intelligence for the last decade. His books have sold in their millions and he regularly delivers seminars around the world. But what is emotional intelligence? In essence, it is the ability to read a situation and to respond to it with emotional understanding. The more complex the situation, the more emotional intelligence is required. Michael Fullan, in Leading in a Culture of Change *(Jossey-Bass, 2001), takes this one step further by explaining that, '[T]he most effective leaders are not the smartest in an IQ sense but are those who combine intellectual brilliance with emotional intelligence.'*

Thinking points

- How well do you know yourself? How do you react when under pressure? Have you asked your colleagues how you are perceived? It is a human trait to revert to basic knee-jerk emotions when under pressure. As a school leader you must understand what creates these pressures and how your 'basic self' reacts in those situations.

- Unlike many professions, being a teacher means dealing with a vast array of emotions which rise and ebb on an almost hourly basis. This emotional roller coaster, generated by the many demands on a teacher, can be exhausting as anyone who has met a teacher on the last day of the summer term will see. There are natural high and low periods during the year that should be carefully monitored so that the emotional mood of the school can be managed.

Tips, ideas and activities

- Stein and Book (*The EQ Edge*, 2000) name five realms of Emotional Intelligence Quotient (EQ):
    1. Intrapersonal (self-awareness, actualisation, independence and self-regard).
    2. Interpersonal (empathy, social responsibility).
    3. Adaptability (problem solving, flexibility).
    4. Stress management (stress tolerance, impulse control).
    5. General mood (happiness, optimism).

They found that teachers who were rigid and lacked impulse were ineffective. Teaching is about relationships and a balance of these five realms supports emotionally intelligent leadership. It stands to reason that where a good leader will strive to improve their understanding of their subject, a good leader will also learn how to improve their EQ to better lead their school.

- How aware are you of your staff's welfare? If you are not able to get into the staffroom, who is acting as your eyes and ears? It is not possible to support an individual if you are not aware they need support, so what strategies do you have in place to ensure that individual need is not overlooked?

- What is your motivation to work? EQ is tightly linked to personal aims and values which, in turn, tie into your personal educational vision.

- Once a year, set time aside with your School Leadership Team (SLT) to perform a review of your performance. Look to identify three strengths to every area of development.

- Below are some websites related to emotional intelligence:
    - www.danielgoleman.info
    - www.eiconsortium.org

You Can... Develop leadership qualities

You Can... Lead professional development

Professional development is relevant to all within education, be they teachers, leaders or teaching assistants. It is about improving your practice, defining your pedagogy and career development. All schools aspire to excellence in teaching and, in order to have excellent teachers, you should aim to cultivate a climate of individualised professional learning. This should reflect individual needs but also meet the demands of the school and curriculum. This is a delicate balance but where a school makes thoughtful investment, it can lead to a win-win scenario for all.

Thinking points

- Hargreaves and Fullan (*Understanding Teacher Development*, 1992) stated that 'Teacher development...involves more than changing teachers behaviour. It also involves changing the person the teachers' is...[a]cknowledging that a teacher's development is also a process of personal development marks an important step forward in our improvement efforts.'

- Professional development has, in recent years, become a business in its own right. Training needs are being met by a range of providers beyond the school's local authority. With such a plethora of options it is easy to fall into the trap of attending a course for the sake of it rather than it meeting your professional needs. However, schools can look to themselves for training and experience. Institutes such as the NCSL are favouring school-based research as opposed to external, out-of-school seminars.

Tips, ideas and activities

- The National College for School Leadership (NCSL) has been at the forefront of leading in education over the last ten years. It offers a wide range of external leadership courses that are, in many cases, accredited and they provide opportunities to reflect upon your current practice. Courses that are run in groups, such as Leadership Pathways, offer opportunities for colleagues to share a learning experience.

- Teachers TV has established itself as a centre for professional development. They have thousands of film clips covering almost every aspect of education. As they are often less than 15 minutes long, these films are ideal for use in twilight training.

- Consider what purpose your Continuing Professional Development (CPD) is serving. Are courses simply driven by educational reform or the fact that they exist? Professional development should be linked to the school's vision which, in turn, should link to individual development.

- Many schools are researching and investing in succession plans by creating teams that are, in theory, self-replacing. These teams offer genuine professional development by exposing colleagues to real-life experiences. Shadow-staff structures, where senior leaders are supported by middle or new leaders, offer similar opportunities. Schools should be mindful that due to the demand for headteachers, deputies are entering headship faster than in the past, which leaves a tier of leadership vacant. These vacancies can provide opportunities for internal promotion.

- Professional development starts the day you walk into a classroom and does not end until you metaphorically close the door behind you on your last day. In an ever-changing environment such as education there is never a time when a school leader can genuinely say 'I know it all.'

You Can... Develop leadership qualities

You Can... **Plan for staff succession**

The chances are that if your school is not strategically planning for senior leadership succession then the one next to you will be. Over the next six years an estimated 25 per cent of all senior leaders will be retiring nationally and in some areas of the country that figure is nearer to 50 per cent. Unfortunately there is not a natural generation to step up to the top jobs, with leadership falling to a younger generation. However, where there is a serious issue there is also the opportunity for these roles and other leadership models to be explored.

Thinking points

- Aside from the present concern surrounding filling the posts, succession plans should form the backbone of all leadership teams. In an age of increasing professional mobility, it is less likely (or even desirable) that senior leaders will remain in one school for long periods. Your governing body should be looking at who are the future leaders within your school and preparing them accordingly.

- Equally, you should be asking yourself at what point you will consider headship. Is it the perception of headship that prevents you from taking on the job or do you simply need a push?

- Potential needs to be identified early on if your school is aiming to grow its own leaders. Encourage aspiring leaders and consider where you could create opportunities for them to lead the school.

Tips, ideas and activities

- What is your leadership structure? Do you link Teaching and Leadership Awards (TLAs) to subjects (as traditionally done) or are they aligned to leadership attributes that are project-driven?

- Does your school have a shadow structure? Shadow structures allow middle and junior leaders the opportunity to work alongside experienced senior leaders. It is also an opportunity to foster future leaders.

- Has your school undertaken extended professional development programmes such as Leading from the Middle (LftM), Leadership Pathways or National Professional Qualification for Headship (NPQH)? These successful programmes have supported thousands of schools and often offer a rare opportunity for teams to reflect on their leadership skills.

- Below is a list of key messages for succession planning:
  1. Have a clear vision – be explicit about what you want.
  2. Be involved – know what is going on in your school.
  3. Lead by example.
  4. Plan for development by investing time and money.
  5. Select well – use and retain existing staff.
  6. Create opportunities and act early – delegate/distribute leadership.
  7. Take risks and trust your staff.
  8. Be prepared to let them fly!

- Governors are also aware that they have a responsibility when it comes to ensuring that there is good leadership within the school. Part of this responsibility is talent spotting, identifying the leaders of tomorrow and providing the resources they need to become that leader.

You Can... Develop a school

You Can... Identify the key characteristics of an effective school

Leadership that promotes change, holds learning as its central value and embraces risk is rarely uniform in style. As school leaders we all bring our own personal flavour and with it our own perception of what schools should look like and to what ethos we would want a child to be exposed. That said, an effective school would expect to show clear vision, a belief in learning, a value of all human resources, respect for its community and an ability to listen to it, and it will be proactive within a risk-taking environment when challenging learning.

Thinking points

- Without exception, the most important resource you will invest in will be your staff. It is with good reason that colleagues should expect clear leadership that respects their value. Appropriate professional development goes towards reinforcing the good characteristics of your school, while coaching colleagues should foster collaborative relationships. The way you are perceived will be based on how you manage these relationships and your ability to relate to people.

- In recent years there has been the inclination to view education through a business lens. While there are good links to be made, education has pupils' learning as its core value, which is significantly different to financial business development. Although value for money must be maintained, as educators we are not in the business of making money and so, to that degree, business characteristics can be flawed and should be embraced with care.

Tips, ideas and activities

- Your learning environment reflects your school characteristics. From your office to your classrooms you should consider what sort of environment you are wishing to display. It does not suit everyone to have a clinically tidy office but if you are more eclectic in your organisation you should consider if you are sufficiently organised to meet your school's needs.

- Home background has a direct influence on schools and therefore learning. Working alongside your community and building a school that reflects their needs, as much as meeting the demands of the National Curriculum, will go towards supporting your pupils' academic performance.

- Children learn best in a fair environment that is both nurturing and disciplined. Consider every aspect of classroom practice and how it relates to these characteristics.

- Below are a number of websites that may be of support:
  - www.ncsl.org.uk (search for the PDF *Effective leadership in multi-ethnic schools*).
  - www.sedl.org/change/leadership/character.html#summ provides an academic evaluation of school characteristics.
  - www.danielgoleman.info develops the main themes of his emotional intelligence.

You Can... Lead an urban school

Urban schools provide a whole host of challenges that can stretch even the most accomplished school leader from high pupil mobility to falling roll numbers or over-subscription. Cultural diversity and ethnic groups require understanding, while sensitivity is required for broken families. Privileged families may live alongside the poorest, and the broadest forms of special need. Yet, faced with this huge challenge, urban leaders have the capacity to lead with vision and the unequivocal aim of securing learning opportunities for all, which often includes staff as well as children.

Thinking points

Urban schools are increasingly hit by what is referred to as the 'London phenomenon'. Simply put, primary catchment areas are often so close to one another that a family can, within good reason, pick and choose where they wish their child to be schooled. It is not uncommon, therefore, for schools that are affected by this to have children leaving to attend a neighbouring school only to return a year or so later. This is unsettling for the child where the parents are lead by the 'grass is greener' philosophy. If you believe your school is affected by this phenomenon then consider what percentage of pupil mobility is attributed to it. Unpicking the reasons why it is occurring may help to dissuade some parents from moving their child and work towards securing a child's stable learning.

Tips, ideas and activities

- Know your school. It's an obvious thing to state but knowing your school includes knowing its history and how it has changed, from staff turnover and community make-up to what educational initiatives it has embraced. Within the last 15 years the cultural make-up of this country has dramatically altered and with it so will your school's. If you know your school you are already well equipped to engage with change.

- Know your subject. To be able to equip children for their futures, today's leaders are required to be serious professionals who have the knowledge and personal capacity to support them. There are a growing number of websites and resources that can help inform you of educational changes and trends. This will give you confidence as a school leader and support successful change within your school.

- Know your staff. Urban teachers tend to be younger than their rural colleagues with different motivations that can include being mobile themselves. As a school leader you should consider what is in it for these teachers. What professional development do you offer? Where do they look for promotions? Is it externally or do you have an established succession plan for all aspects of leadership within your school, particularly senior positions?

- Know yourself. Leading an inner-city school is as rewarding as it is challenging. In an environment where no two hours, let alone two days, are the same, you will be required to demonstrate a sincere depth of character which has energy and enthusiasm.

You Can... Develop a school

You Can... **Lead a small school**

Small schools are often told they cost too much. Yet, for their size, they offer great value for money, which is borne out in test results and inspection reports. In 2005 the Commission for the Countryside reported that schools with 100 or less on roll, including very small schools, did better than larger primaries. The commitment of small-school leaders is to be commended and offers genuine opportunities for experimental leadership models.

Thinking points

- The majority of small schools (those with fewer than 100 pupils) are within rural settings. The consequences of this are smaller budgets, fewer staff and greater responsibilities on those staff members' shoulders. A headteacher in a small school is likely to find themselves teaching (an independent study suggests that 40 per cent of headteachers have at least five hours a week teaching commitment) as well as wearing a wide range of curricular 'hats'.

- Small schools have much greater experience of networking than their inner-city colleagues. It could be argued that there is a need to network in order to share resources and ideas but their experiences of what works well could be shared with larger schools that are just beginning to network.

Tips, ideas and activities

- Don't try to reinvent the wheel. If you are writing a policy, first ask members within your network learning community for examples or search the internet.

- Share skills and experience. Although it is not always possible to release teachers from the classroom, they could be available to run shared twilight training.

- Recruiting senior leaders, particularly headteachers, can be challenging as it is not possible to offer the same level salary that is available in larger schools. As a significant percentage of current headteachers are reaching retirement over the next six years, other models of leadership may have to be investigated, particularly federated schools. Federation formally creates a network that is supervised by a single headteacher (similar to the American system).

- A small school has a greater capacity to change quickly as the headteacher will tend to have a much more personal relationship with the children, their families and community. When addressing change, such as tackling low-level disruptive behaviour, involve the wider community. Your chances of success will improve with a wider range of stakeholders buying into your vision.

- The leadership skills needed for a small school are no different from those in different circumstances. The approach may differ but at heart will be your passion for teaching combined with your vision for learning.

- Small-school leaders are eligible for allowances to support professional development on programmes such as National Professional Qualification for Headship (NPQH), Leading from the Middle and Leadership Pathways.

You Can... **Develop a school**

You Can... Plan a budget

A clearly managed budget should support the school, helping it to identify need and, where that has been done, to make strategic plans to meet those needs based on the known financial constraints. Simply put, you can't spend what you don't have, which is where school leaders need to be creative. Understanding your budget will help you to anticipate where there are financial gaps and therefore give you time to look for solutions.

Thinking points

- Budget systems are about to be overhauled. Historically, a school could expect an audit every six years or so. However, with the onset of FMSiS (Financial Management Standard in Schools) schools should prepare themselves for a three-year rolling programme: FMSiS inspection in year one, year two to address any issues and year three for a standard audit before the cycle resumes. Although the learning curve may be steep at the start, the programme should support schools with long-term financial planning.

- Bursars are increasingly recognised as key to helping schools make better use of their resources and facilities. Sometimes referred to as the school business manager, a good bursar can lift the responsibility of financial management from the School Leadership Team, who can then place it within a strategic educational framework.

- Finances within small schools are often much tighter than in full two- or three-form entry schools. In this case it is possible to share a bursar between schools.

Tips, ideas and activities

- Ensure you have up-to-date signatories and that they are aware of this responsibility. Signatories within school should extend no further than members of staff in the most senior positions.

- Governors' financial meetings can be weighty. That said, do not forget the smallest items such as signing and dating minutes from the previous meeting, which could be picked up during an audit.

- Schools and children's centres are being progressively encouraged to project budgets over the next three years. Within this projection, schools should have room to indicate planned expenditures such as replacing the ICT suite or future personnel appointments.

- Know how your budget is formulated. Although there are now three census days, it is during the January census that pupil figures are taken in order to calculate your budget. Each child has a financial weighting and it is not uncommon for schools to experience pupil mobility at this time as competing establishments find they are able to offer places.

- Be mindful of the various starts and ends of year. As educators we are conditioned to work from September to July but financial years run from April to March. Although you may be familiar with this, your colleagues may not and, as a result, might have a different set of spending expectations that should be sensitively addressed.

- Websites that may be of support include:
  - www.fmsis.info
  - www.ncsl.org.uk (NCSL offers programmes for school business managers/bursars).

You Can... **Develop a vision**

The concept of a whole-school vision as opposed to having a set of aims and values is very much a 21st century idea. As a result, developing one is a relatively new venture for most schools and while it may be true that many primary schools now subscribe to a vision of some kind or other, it may be the first time they have tied their school to one. A good vision fastens together a school's values and aims with the community's dreams for tomorrow. A vision should show daring, creativity and challenge. It should also be succinct so that it doesn't get lost within itself.

Thinking points

- There are two ways of leading a vision. Either the vision is a set path for direction or it is a set of guiding principles for future change. There is strength in both approaches as long as you monitor progress, thereby ensuring you are working towards an agreed set of common goals to improve standards.

- Vision equals change and change can be uncomfortable. As a school leader it is your responsibility to identify what obstacles may conflict with the vision so that sensitive and reasonable steps can be taken to embrace the whole community.

- A vision takes time to realise and once done it should be justly celebrated (even if it has changed during its journey, which is often inevitable). It is also an appropriate time to evaluate its impact and to determine how, if it is appropriate, the vision should evolve for the next phase of the school's life.

Tips, ideas and activities

- Establishing a community's vision takes time. If you are considering writing your first vision statement, assign it as a school improvement priority for your school year. This will establish the vision development as a core priority with colleagues and governors. It is, however, a useful exercise to undertake if you are relatively new to the establishment (but get to know your school first before launching into a new vision).

- Establish a working party. This team should cross all sections of the school such as a school leader, a teacher, a governor and a parent or parent governor. As well as assigning responsibilities and roles this team, as a cross section, will help you to gain a 360-degree understanding of the school.

- Be mindful of whom you are consulting. You should consider appropriate methods of consultation for all staff members, children, governors, parents, other groups involved with the community and the local authority. This will give a focused result that reflects a common thought.

- Surveys, particularly online surveys, are a quick way of collecting hard evidence to support opinions, but for in-depth knowledge you will need to consider a range of face-to-face opportunities. These may include staff meetings, individual staff consultations, meetings with the school council, parent-school partnership families and other stakeholders such as meal supervisors and teaching assistants.

- Keep the profile of the vision high. Public meetings could be arranged in the playground, during parent consultation evenings or before whole-school events such as harvest festival where there will naturally be a large number of parents on-site.

- Below are some of websites that may be of support:
  - www.surveymonkey.com
  - www.nsba.org/sbot/toolkit/cav.html

You Can... **Develop a school**

You Can... Complete a robust Self-Evaluation Form

Since 2006 schools have been required to keep an up-to-date school self-review, or Self-Evaluation Form (SEF). This review document is designed to inform an Ofsted inspection team and direct the school inspection under the new framework for inspection. It is not meant to be a descriptive history of the school but a robust document that is both current and analytical.

Thinking points

- As with most areas of school life, a SEF requires management. There are natural times of the year when it makes sense to update different sections. See pages 59–61 for a timetable of school events, including suggested times to update different SEF sections. This is only a suggestion but can support the management and distribute the workload that the SEF presents.

- At heart, the SEF is an evaluative assessment of current practice. It is not the vision of the school and should not be used to drive the vision. It is true that the SEF may reveal aspects of review that may be sufficiently significant to form an area for short-term school improvement but should not be used as the central vehicle for long-term vision implementation.

Tips, ideas and activities

- When writing SEF sections make sure you are responding to the question. It is good practice to work with a team (usually made up of your School Leadership Team (SLT) but it is also an opportunity to involve a governor) to review the document. Keep asking yourself if you have answered the question and if your answer is concise and accurate.

- A consistent writer's voice is important throughout the document and does not have to be the responsibility of the headteacher. If the deputy or assistant headteacher writes clearer English, consider delegating the role to them. This will also go towards ensuring that a broader range of leaders have a corporate understanding of the school.

- The SEF is a joint responsibility and should be communicated to the whole staff at least once a year. Where there are areas of responsibility, such as the Foundation Stage or extended schools, the area leader should provide the evidence for that section.

- Ofsted recommends that before you submit your SEF you should consider the following points:
    1. Have you read it through?
    2. Is it short and to the point?
    3. Have you answered all of the questions?
    4. Are your judgements clear?
    5. Have you reflected stakeholders' views?
    6. Does it give a fair and honest picture of what the school is like?
    7. Have you been clear about actions being taken to improve?
    8. If you were an inspector what questions would your SEF lead you to ask?

- A document written by Ofsted may help when you are writing your SEF. Visit www.ofsted.gov.uk (search for the document *Writing a SEF that works*).

You Can... Develop a school

You Can... Work with the media

In the modern world it is increasingly likely that at some point you will be required to talk to a journalist. Although this may fill you with horror, the reality is that in most cases the media is on the school's side and is looking to support you. A good headteacher will have a firm hold on what potential the media has, be it web-based blogs, radio or TV interviews, and will use it to promote the school.

Thinking points

We are still in a communications revolution. Over the last 15 years our ability and speed to communicate has altered beyond all recognition. Along with it so have our attitudes about how we communicate. Social networks, such as Facebook™ or MySpace®, and blogs now communicate as much energy as phone calls and we are only now beginning to understand their real impact on socialising. Already, teachers socialise on Facebook™ and it won't be long before other, more formal, communication can be passed through these methods.

Tips, ideas and activities

- Cultivate your relationship with the local Press. Invite them to 'get to know you' meetings and keep them abreast of newsworthy events. It is more likely that they will support the school if sudden news breaks when there is a working relationship.

- Create a media working party. Major businesses have press officers who manage any media attention; a team of governors, parents and teachers can act in the same way.

- When you are planning your school year, identify key events that might interest the Press. The better your relationship, the quicker you will be at identifying newsworthy stories.

- Teacher's TV is often looking for innovative ideas to film. It is worth contacting them with any areas that you feel are of excellence or innovation.

- Promote internal success. If one of your teachers is a writer or an artist then celebrate their personal success.

- Don't be scared of picking up the phone. The local Press, contrary to popular belief, wants to support local activities, which includes those in schools. They will be delighted to hear from you.

- Design a website. Keep it simple so that it does not need regular updating. Attend the annual BETT Conference (held at Olympia in January) to meet the latest web designers. They are often more reasonable than you would think!

- TeacherNet provides a useful document that, although aimed at London secondary schools, offers good advice. Visit http://publications.teachernet.gov.uk (search for the PDF document *A media toolkit for secondary schools*).

You Can... **Develop a school**

You Can... Delegate

Delegation is a core characteristic of successful leadership. The challenge is knowing at what level to delegate. Arguably there are times when delegation skills are required, which depend on a range of factors including finances, human resources and time. But delegation delivers a strong message, it says, 'I trust you – go and do it'. However, in its crudest terms, if it is not sincere then delegation can be a form of manipulation, which in turn can be demoralising. When delegating you should consider what powers are being delegated and for what purpose.

Thinking points

- Delegation can provide genuine professional development opportunities. If you are considering delegating a responsibility you must first identify the person to whom it will be delegated. It may be that a handover period is required, depending on the colleague's experience, and appropriate support should be provided with clear milestones.

- Delegate evenly. It is easy to fall into the trap of delegating to colleagues who are either competent or willing. Although there is some truth in the staffroom metaphor that there are energy creators and energy consumers within a workforce, well-pointed delegation can create its own climate of change tolerance, which in turn will support the long term vision of the school.

Tips, ideas and activities

- Professor Tim Brighouse, former London Schools Commissioner, sets out nine levels of delegation ranging from the pure autocrat to the genuine democrat. This spectrum can be used as a personal indicator of your leadership stance. There is no question that there are times when clear, directed leadership is needed but being aware of the spectrum is helpful for your own professional development as well as for your colleagues. The genuine delegator should be working towards levels 7–9 on the spectrum.
    1. Look into this problem. Give me all the facts. I will decide what to do.
    2. Let me know the options available with the pros and cons of each. I will decide which to select.
    3. Let me know the criteria for your recommendation, which alternatives you have identified and which one appears best to you, with any risk identified. I will make the decision.
    4. Recommend a course of action for my approval.
    5. Let me know what you intend to do. Delay action until I approve.
    6. Let me know what you intend to do. Do it unless I say not to.
    7. Take action. Let me know what you did. Let me know how it turns out.
    8. Take action. Communicate with me only if action is unsuccessful.
    9. Take action. No further communication with me is necessary.

Brighouse adds a note of caution. He states that 'The surest way of consuming energy and demoralising and disempowering staff is to tell them you are at number seven but, at the height of a crisis, tell them subsequently you were really at number five!' Be true to yourself.

- Download a copy of *How successful headteachers survive and thrive* at: www.rm.com

You Can... Develop a school

You Can... Implement a School Improvement Plan

Core improvement requires management and development if it is to have a significant impact on learners and the learning environment. There may be seasonal conditions to be aware of or financial implications. Take into consideration who will be responsible for key actions, that the school is on board and that you have the resources (financial, time and physical) to implement your plan. If this is in place you have improved your chances of long-term impact.

Thinking points

- Governors are central to how improvement is identified and managed through the School Improvement Plan. Although there is no legal requirement, the Guide to the Law for School Governors states that 'A good governing body will ensure that the school has in place an effective process for reviewing performance, identifying priorities, taking action and monitoring progress.'

- School Improvement Plans are increasingly linked to school financial management. The DCSF Financial Management Standard in Schools ((FMSiS), see page 17 and www.standards.dcsf.gov.uk/vfm/leadership/siplanning) discretely ties finances to school development. It is an important strategy that allows school leaders to map school improvement priorities meaningfully against known available funds.

Tips, ideas and activities

- The School Improvement Plan (SIP) has a natural cycle of implementation, action and evaluation. Typically it will run for one year, covering 15 months of development:
    - April to June – School Leadership Team (SLT) and governors discuss areas for development.
    - June to July – present key areas for development to governing body and staff body.
    - September – complete action plans for the coming year to present to the curriculum committee.
    - October to May – core period for action.
    - June to July – evaluate key areas for improvement, overlapping the development period for the next academic year.

- A School Improvement Plan should have no more than six focus areas of which:
    - One should relate to standards within a core curriculum.
    - One should focus on a foundation subject (ideally two foundation subjects should be reviewed each year which would allow for all foundation subjects to be highlighted over a four-year rolling programme).
    - One should reflect an area of development that is part of the vision plan.

- All plans should be written in an agreed format with an agreed font and writing style. They should not be descriptive. See page 62 for a suggested format.

- Plans should clearly lay out milestones and action that needs to be taken in order for the overall objective to be met. An action plan should aim to be no more than two or three pages in length.

- Action plans can roll over. If the work has taken longer then that should be recorded and the action plan adapted accordingly.

You Can... **Develop a school**

You Can... Work with your School Improvement Partner

In 2005, a new phrase began to be circulated – 'the single conversation'. This single conversation referred to a bringing together of corporate fragments that schools are involved with such as health, local authority, finance and child protection. Different grants were dramatically reduced, red tape cut, the opportunity for three-year budget plans introduced, online publication instead of the flood of posted literature, school self-evaluation introduced and a dramatic change to Ofsted inspections. Along with this, link advisors were replaced by School Improvement Partners (SIPs).

Thinking points

- Within the original DfES, 2005 publication *A New Relationship with Schools: Next Steps* the single conversation was unpicked: 'This single conversation' brings into alignment several interactions that many schools have hitherto experienced as separate, fragmented discussions. In particular, it brings together the discussions about schools' future plans and targets, about the support schools need from outside, about re-designation for specialist school status, about local authorities' categorisation of schools, about head teachers' performance, and about the follow-up to Ofsted reports.'

- SIPs are not tied to one authority and are effectively freelance. In many cases SIPs are lead professionals and will often be substantive headteachers. They will understand your challenges and offer genuine experience.

Tips, ideas and activities

- Ensure that both you and your SIP understand what is being asked – don't be afraid to question your SIP for clarification.

- Set aside ring-fenced time. Your SIP meetings are your opportunity to get to grips with wider school issues.

- Your SIP is not your confidant and may act as devil's advocate when questioning you. Be prepared.

- You are entitled to five SIP visits a year with an optional sixth that can form either a report for the governors or a SIP presentation. The DCSF document *School Improvement Partner Reports* (2007) includes a diagram showing the available sections that a SIP will comment upon.

- Read the SIP report. It should be clear and free from educational jargon. The report will be read by non-professionals such as governors so will need to be accessible. Allow for some flexibility of focus on the reports; avoid a cyclical pattern of practice.

- Your SIP will change every two to three years. A new SIP should be able to pick up from the previous one.

- All SIP reports should be ready for circulation within good time after the visit, generally within two weeks.

- The documents suggested below may help when first working with a School Improvement Partner. Go to http://publications.teachernet.gov.uk (search for the documents *A New Relationship with Schools: Next steps* and *School Improvement Partner reports*).

You Can... Develop a school

You Can... **Plan for Ofsted**

By 2009, all primary schools will have experienced an inspection under the new framework for inspections. Typically schools are given 48-hours notice before an inspection, which now centres around the school Self-Evaluation Form ((SEF), see page 19). Most teachers would expect to receive a short lesson observation lasting around fifteen minutes with feedback given immediately. The basis of the inspection is that you know your school and not, as it was perceived previously, the inspection team looking to tell you about your school.

Thinking points

- Fundamentally, Ofsted are looking for answers to two questions: 1. What are the academic standards and how are they achieved? and 2. How is the school led in all its leadership forms (such as governors, senior leaders and middle leaders)? If you are able to answer these by drawing upon your SEF and other documents then you will be well-placed for your inspection.

- School leaders instinctively know when they are due an inspection. If your school was inspected in 2007 then it stands to reason that during 2010 you should expect another visit (it may be a light touch, which would have been indicated from your last visit, in which case this will only be one day). Prepare your staff, governors and yourself appropriately. Get your ship in order.

Tips, ideas and activities

- Review your SEF. Look carefully at the questions it asks and answer them directly.

- Review your last inspection report as it may have items in it that are current. Evaluate any action taken.

- Judge the type of inspection you are expecting. If it is a light touch then prepare yourself rigorously. Consider what aspects may be discussed, which colleagues should be observed and brief your senior colleagues, staff and governors.

- Do not panic! Unlike the old system where an inspection was preceded by half a term of anxiety, this new system is, in its simplest form, looking at how well you know your school.

- Be calm. Your staff will be looking to you to lead them.

- Inform your chair of governors and staff.

- Ensure that your documentation and systems are known by all senior leaders who may need to locate information for an inspection.

- Identify a suitable place for the team to work and ensure that all documentation is available.

- Be professional, succinct in conversation and answer their questions. Challenge appropriately and provide supporting evidence.

- Support your colleagues once the inspection has been completed and celebrate success.

- Lightning (no notice) inspections are being discussed. Your School Leadership Team will need to understand the school in a similar depth to you because the next senior leader will have to manage the inspection if you are absent.

You Can... **Develop a school**

You Can... Empower your community to embrace educational risk

Being an educational risk-taker should not generate pictures of teachers encouraging children to leap off desks simply to prove the force of gravity. A school that embraces risks looks at how they can create a dynamic learning environment that is supported by the community and meets the needs of the individual learner. It may mean changes within the curriculum, physical adaptations to the building or structural changes to the staffing. A school that embraces educational risk can use it as a compelling creative motivator for learning.

Thinking points

- Learning behaviour comes from a learning need. Where there is need, there requires a change in pedagogical stance to meet it. For both the learner and teacher, risk-taking involves change, which can be uncomfortable. However, if the teacher can identify that the behaviour is arising from a need, then identifying what that need is will work towards supporting the individual learner and improve their chances of success. In short, one shoe does not fit all and learning environments must be flexible at all levels.

- Risk-taking should have a clear rationale and reflect the feelings of the school community. For example, it may be that your school is reviewing the curriculum and wishes to teach all of its Speaking and listening through performance. If this meets the needs of the National Curriculum and reflects the feelings of the school community, then such a risk will be minimal.

Tips, ideas and activities

- Consult your school body. What makes for exciting learning? Children, parents and staff will all have different ideas and good consultation should help identify areas of commonality as well as revealing fresh opportunities.

- Does your vision embrace open-ended opportunities for learning?

- Professional development should be identified to support any major changes to pedagogical practice.

- Since the publication of *Excellence and Enjoyment* (DfES 2003), schools have been given licence to adapt the learning programme as they see fit. By 2010 there will have been a substantial review of the current National Curriculum, which will further open opportunities for learning.

- How do you use ICT to enhance learning? Schools are used to interactive whiteboards but ICT has moved from the board into the pocket. The internet is now available on most mobile phones. This generation of children have an intimate knowledge of the web – they literally were born into it – and schools need to play a creative game of catch-up if they are to truly meet modern children's ICT aspirations.

- Celebrate creativity within the school.

- The website below may help when embracing educational risk:
  - http://www.ncsl.org.uk (search for *Developing creativity for learning in the primary school*).

You Can... **Develop a school**

You Can... Lead in the future

Planning for the future can sound exhausting when each year presents its own challenges. However, as our primary role is to prepare today's children for tomorrow we must look to what tomorrow may bring. Issues such as climate change and technology will have significant impact on this generation. The better we can envision the future, the greater the chance that our children will have the necessary skills to meet it.

Thinking points

- How prepared for the future are you? Does your vision of the school look beyond five years? What resources are likely to change? Have you enough capacity to manage succession where it is necessary? Is there somebody prepared to take on your job and do they have the necessary skills?

- As school leaders, we spend the majority of our time fire-fighting or managing the mountain of initiatives that land in our in-trays. Time must be taken out of the schedule for reflection and direction. Different schools find different models useful, however, aim to spend quality time, off-site, with key leaders (including the chair of governors) to review and plan for the future. If your budget allows it, plan for an overnight stay in a hotel away from school. This will dramatically reduce the potential distractions and allow you to spend some social time with colleagues.

Tips, ideas and activities

- Leadership has changed dramatically over the last ten years and will, in all likelihood, continue with its evolution.

- Consider how involved your community is in the school and how involved you are in the community.

- Schools will increasingly work in partnerships, such as with children's centres, extended schools providers, local school networks and other informal agreements. What systems do you have in place to manage and lead these groups?

- Leadership is set to change within schools. Where schools once led through subjects it is increasingly common to see schools creating project leaders. The Teaching and Learning Responsibility (TLR) point system allows for this – is it something you have discussed with your School Leadership Team?

- Are you aware of what the political parties are planning? Although the last ten years have been ten years of great change, they have been very stable through the virtue of one political party. This will not last forever and, as a school, you must have a concept of what impact a different party might have on your establishment.

- What sort of leader are you? What are your personal aspirations? Do you have the skills to meet these aspirations? Planning your personal leadership is as important as planning the school's.

- We haven't got a crystal ball. However much we try to plan for the future, we cannot plan for everything. All we can do is our best by learning from change and challenge.

You Can... Lead learning and teaching

You Can... Develop your curriculum

The curriculum is the beating heart of the school and the backbone for all learning. How you manage your curriculum dictates the educational flavour of your pupils' learning and also establishes what, as a school leader, you believe is the learning purpose. It will inevitably reflect your personal interests, be it sports or literature, but smart leadership will have a finger on the pulse of the community and will aim to reflect it in the learning opportunities given to the children.

Thinking points

- However you address your curriculum, the end result will be measured standards, which must demonstrate that your children have attained age-appropriate levels or above. This can be met through a creative curriculum and there is little doubt that children can have life-changing experiences through performance and explorative learning opportunities. That said, you cannot take your eye off the ball. If your standards are good, the next question will always be 'How can you make them better?'

- The only statutory curriculum document that we, as teachers, must adhere to is the National Curriculum. Over the last decade the Primary National Strategies have been developed for maths and literacy to support learning but these documents are not statutory and some schools have opted not to use them. Indeed, if we are to look at alternative ways of leading then international curriculums, such as those of Australia and New Zealand, offer an interesting perspective on some areas of learning.

Tips, ideas and activities

- The curriculum is not a fixed point of reference. It is in flux and will reflect the social and political norms of the day. As a result, you should prepare yourself for a review of your curriculum every three to four years. It may be just a tweaking of the original but it gives an opportunity for the leadership team to take stock of what topics their children are learning.

- Curricular reviews may be enforced by change (such as with the renewed frameworks for maths and literacy). This can be anticipated by keeping both an eye on current reviews (such as the primary curriculum review, see page 57) and by attending briefing meetings.

- Involve your children in curriculum development. Extended schools offers a great opportunity to run classes that do not fit the standard day, such as specialised sports or arts classes, and can meet the needs of your learners. By 2010 all schools must offer or be able to direct people to a local establishment that supports an extended day of 8am–6pm, 48 weeks a year.

- Curriculum review is a substantial task and would, arguably, form an element of your School Improvement Plan (SIP).

- How does your curriculum embrace the *Every Child Matters* agenda? Again, it may not be discretely through day-to-day lessons but the *Every Child Matters* objectives should form the heart of how learning is approached.

- Below are some useful websites linking to the curriculum:
    - http://curriculum.qca.org.uk
    - www.google.co.uk/intl/en/schools/index.html

You Can... **Lead learning and teaching**

You Can... Manage behaviour

Managing behaviour is a challenge for all schools in varying degrees. It is an aspect that Ofsted takes very seriously as does every parent, child and teacher. If behaviour is poor, the finger, unfortunately, will eventually point to the top with the inevitable question: What are you going to do about it? So, you must ask yourself: What do we do about it and what can we do better?

Thinking points

- Behaviour policies should be reviewed every three years in order to keep them current. The review provides an opportunity to involve your children with the process. Children have a very clear view of what is good or bad behaviour and will naturally want to seek adult assurance while supporting their friends. A jointly-agreed policy will help children to better understand the procedures. This can then be shared will their peers.

- There is no golden formula for low-level persistently poor behaviour and this must be communicated to the parent(s). It is the duty of the school to support young learners so that they can maximise the opportunities given to them and that can call for creative thinking. If one idea seems to stop working this is not a failure, it is simply time to think of a new idea to keep behaviour in check.

Tips, ideas and activities

- Your behaviour policy should be a single message that you can sell to everybody. It should be an accessible, clear distillation of what adults and children think is reasonable behaviour.

- Everybody should have a clear understanding of what your behaviour policy and strategies are, from class teachers to meal supervisors and teaching assistants. Policies break down when people do not know or adhere to the systems that support the policies.

- Celebrate good behaviour. Hold a monthly 'good behaviour' assembly and showcase your 'behaviour-heroes' to the school.

- Children respond to positive behaviour. If a class is loud and they need to be quiet then praise those children who are ready. They will all soon quieten down – even if it's an assembly of children!

- Behavioural problems can begin when children are bored, such as at lunch times. If this is the case then employing key children to perform tasks, such as older children being a play-buddy to younger ones, will divert any opportunities for inappropriate behaviour.

- In 2007 the Government launched, Social and Emotional Aspects of Learning (SEAL) as a programme to help teach primary-aged children about the importance of emotions within social situations and the impact of emotions on learning. Schools that have started to use SEAL have often done so in place of PSHE lessons.

- Websites to support schools dealing with behaviour issues include:
  - www.standards.dcsf.gov.uk/primary/publications/banda/seal
  - www.pbis.org

You Can... **Lead learning and teaching**

You Can... Ensure quality staff welfare

Staff well-being has begun to be taken seriously and it became part of the workforce remodelling structure of the Excellence and Enjoyment document (DfES) in 2003. Personal life can have a great impact on the day-to-day work life. Embedded well-being systems can support individual staff members and, consequently, the school, when difficult times occur. School leaders should show due care to their staff as well as the children. After all, your members of staff are your most expensive resource and should be cared for accordingly.

Thinking points

- There will be times of highly intensive work when you will be working around the clock. It is part of the job and your family, as well as yourself, will have to be fully aware of the demands before you start. It is highly rewarding and stimulating but the demands must be respected and understood. Keeping your family informed of peak periods of work will help them to support you.

- All staff with children under the age of 16 have the right to request shorter working hours. Unless there is a very good reason, your governing body should agree to it. In these cases you must keep in mind that, unless the contract has been changed, the employee can request a return to full working hours and the filled vacancy will have to be shed.

Tips, ideas and activities

- All staff members are entitled to buy into nursery voucher schemes. These vouchers are taken off their gross salary and therefore are of greater value than paying directly. Your local authority will be able to arrange this.

- A bit of pampering, such as hiring somebody to massage shoulders or manicure nails can be a relatively inexpensive way of demonstrating value. Equally, termly-arranged breakfasts can cost less than £50 and are a fun way to start the day.

- There is a range of well-being packages available that schools and individuals can buy into. These packages offer financial, legal and practical leadership advice and support. Often included is a health-related MOT. Your local well-being officer will be able to advise you on the package.

- Links with health centres will demonstrate that you value health. Most local authority clubs and many private clubs will offer business or local authority rates. Although it is beyond the means of most schools to pay for monthly subscriptions they could cover the initial enrolment payment.

- Class budgets are an acknowledgement of the investment that many teachers voluntarily put into children's learning. Within business it would never be expected for employees to pay for work-related resources. A £50 class budget could be seen as an act of goodwill.

- Professional development is broadening its scope. Increasingly colleagues are being offered accredited and meaningful Continuing Professional Development (CPD) opportunities. Within the private sector it is a long-established means of retention; colleagues stay for the time taken to complete a subsidised Masters degree.

- PPA arrangements and leadership time can be taken at home where there are often fewer disruptions.

You Can... Observe adults teaching

Each day, across the world, thousands of lessons are being taught to children who are, in the main, willing learners. Yet, it is important to remember that an experienced teacher who has taught many thousands of lessons, may have only had a handful of their lessons observed by another adult. Only within the last ten years have specialists been celebrated and professional development through lesson observation been regarded as worthy as an external course (indeed, in many cases worthier).

Thinking points

- When observing a lesson consider your personal impact on the class. Aim to keep attention on you to a minimum so to gain as true an understanding of the class as is practicable.

- When asking a colleague to perform an observation, consider their experience and competence. If they have little or no lesson observation experience, either arrange to observe a lesson with them or mentor them with an experienced colleague.

- A teacher is entitled to raise a complaint about any part of the observation procedure. In the first instance the headteacher should attempt to resolve the complaint informally. If the matter is not satisfactorily resolved then the teacher is entitled to invoke the school's grievance procedures.

Tips, ideas and activities

- When planning an observation take into consideration:
  - The purpose of the observation, for example, subject review, performance management or NQT observation.
  - The focus of the observation, for example, management of pupils' behaviour or use of ICT (the observation may have a performance management link).
  - The amount of notice given before an observation (five working days is a minimum and with performance management observations the time for these should have been decided at the initial meeting).
  - The length of time of the observation (bear in mind that an Ofsted inspector is likely to spend less than 30 minutes observing a lesson).
  - What information you require, such as the lesson plan.
  - The nature of any judgements made and how they will be recorded and graded, if appropriate.
  - How feedback will be given, written or oral, and when.
  - How the information about the lesson will be used, and whether or not the name of the person being observed will be written on any record of the observation.
  - Who the information about the lesson will be reported to.
  - Whether or not the information will be stored. If so, where and in what form?

- When feeding back after a lesson, always ask the teacher how they felt the lesson went. Invariably they will identify the same strengths and areas for development you have.

- Aim to balance feedback with 80 per cent praise and 20 per cent areas for development. Be honest, but not brutally honest.

- Ultimately lessons are verified by Ofsted. They will be expecting you to know your staff and will test your grades during an inspection. For this reason, although you may have your own grade system, it is important that you can match observations against the Ofsted grades.

You Can... Lead performance management for all

Performance management is the process of assessing a colleague's overall performance against professional standards. These standards are the backdrop to discussions allowing colleagues to engage with relevant data, school improvement priorities and their own personal professional development. Renewed policy guidelines were introduced in 2007 and schools should ensure that their practice is transparent and consistently applied in line with these guidelines. It also offers time to talk to colleagues about their practice and aspirations – a rare opportunity in the busy world of teaching.

Thinking points

- Although performance management has been developed for teaching and leadership staff, its basic principles are transferable to other teams within your school, particularly teaching assistants. It demonstrates that you value their contribution and can help identify where training is required.

- Performance management meetings should be held in a calm, private part of school. They are an opportunity for colleagues to raise issues where there is no other forum to do so. Although there is a tight agenda to go through, there should be time allowed to discuss any extra issues raised.

- Performance management can be linked to pay, particularly if a colleague is crossing a threshold or on the leadership scale. Schools' policies differ around the country but, in essence, crossing a threshold is not automatic and therefore does not necessarily equate to an automatic pay rise.

Tips, ideas and activities

- Performance management meetings for teaching staff can now take place as part of a whole school training day, thereby reducing supply costs.

- Ensure all your team leaders are properly trained and that they understand how to word objectives that are measurable (often referred to as SMART objectives). These objectives should be linked to the School Improvement Plan (SIP).

- Be clear what the targets will be. They must be quantifiable and should reflect the SIP.

- Identify a single objective that ties into the SIP, typically related to a curricular subject. This will give genuine meaning to the SIP for all members of staff and ensure that everyone is driving in the same direction.

- At the initial performance management meeting, set dates for any observations. Only one is required and this typically occurs in the spring term.

- Performance management data can be used when colleagues are considering crossing the threshold or as evidence for accreditations such as Charted London Teacher or National Professional Qualification for Headship. Where possible look for these natural opportunities to dovetail work.

- Observations should carefully reflect the agreed objectives, as discussed in your initial meeting. Remind your colleague of any observations at least a week before.

- It is good practice to hold a mid-year meeting with your colleagues to review progress and to understand what strategies they are going to use or have modified for the rest of the year.

You Can... **Lead learning and teaching**

You Can... Track pupil progress

If standards are the end goal of education then tracking is the central skill needed for monitoring the success of this. The SEF (Self-Evaluation Form) requires the school to address standards by unpicking its tracking procedures so that where there are target groups or trends, the school is aware of what or who they are and has applied the appropriate resources for support. The level of detail required for meaningful intervention is so precise that handwritten tracking is no longer sufficient. Over the last few years a number of electronic tracking tools have been developed to support schools.

Thinking points

- Understanding how to interpret an electronic device is challenging enough even if you know how to interrogate spreadsheets. If you do not have this initial skill then further training is required so that the user is not alienated before they even turn on the computer.

- What do you want the program to do for you? It is tempting to be seduced by reports and 'wizard analysis' but at the end of the day your school is individual and requires individualised tracking. There is no one blueprint. Knowing this, consider what the program can do and ask yourself if it is providing the information you require. If not, how can you get it? It may be a case of using the electronic data in partnership with good old paper and pencil.

Tips, ideas and activities

- RAISEonline was developed to replace PANDA (Ofsted's Performance and Assessment report) and offers an interactive version of past paper-based reports. It is the electronic tracker that an Ofsted team will look at before an inspection, not your own independent tool. Electronic trackers are dependent on data and the level of detail they can provide improves over time. If your school is new to using this type of tool it is important to remember that the value of the data will take around 12–18 months to appreciate.

- Governors should be aware of what tools the school is using to track standards. A presentation at a meeting may be something to consider.

- There is a natural cycle to data logging and analysis. Data is typically collected at hand-over meetings in July, October, February and June.

- How can teachers access the data? Is it from a suite of computers or just one laptop? Availability may be an issue.

- Do you have a back-up of the data? In most cases the data can easily fit onto a memory stick but a back-up should be made after every significant update of the program.

- A refined assessment programme, Assessing Pupils' Progress (APP), was introduced across the country in 2008 with an implementation date of 2009. The argument for APP was that national and local data was showing that a significant number of pupils were not making satisfactory progress during a key stage, with some pupils becoming stuck or regressing during some stages in their education. APP sets out to refine assessment procedures to bridge these gaps. APP only works if there is a consistent approach within your school with standardisation and moderation forming a central role in quality assurance.

You Can... Work with stakeholders

You Can... Have an effective School Leadership Team

School Leadership Teams (SLTs) are evolving. Just over five years ago the term SLT would have been rarely heard, the older style SMT (Senior Management Team) being the preferred acronym. Although it could be argued that the change comes down to semantics, the message is clear: we are about leading. This message is reflected in the types of professional development available to help equip our senior leaders for the demands of a new learning environment (see page 12). Evolution takes time but what the process offers is dynamic opportunities for fresh leadership models.

Thinking points
- Michael Fullan wrote in *Leading in a Culture of Change* (Jossey-Bass, 2001) that 'ultimately, your leadership in a culture of change will be judged as effective or ineffective not by who you are as a leader, but by what leadership you produce in others'.

- An anxiety shared by many school leaders is the need to challenge when there is a problem. Nobody wants to be reflected in a negative light but as the ability to challenge is a key part of leadership it should be something that is utilised. The problem may be hidden, for example, a person who is self-motivated may appear to be a great asset to the school but their self-motivation might be the result of resisting delegation of tasks to another person). You will have to consider the wisest way to unveil such issues and once they are addressed, this can give colleagues the freedom to act, where in the past they would have side-stepped a problem for the sake of a calm life.

Tips, ideas and activities
- It is a useful exercise to audit the skills base of your SLT. Ask the group to do it on behalf of each other; colleagues will often identify skills that are not personally recognised. Do not fall into the trap of highlighting what they can't do.

- Does your SLT reflect the school body? If not, where are the gaps and what measures can you take to ensure those gaps become filled?

- Education has become an increasingly mobile profession and over the next five years many more 'top' roles will be created (heads of children's centres as well as headteachers). Do your SLT members have the capacity to step up to new roles if your deputy leaves?

- Keep SLT meetings to a reasonable length. Any longer than ninety minutes after school will not be productive. At each meeting appoint one person to take minutes.

- Arrange for governors to occasionally attend SLT meetings to create a working relationship between the two groups.

- Plan your SLT meetings ahead of time. There is a natural cycle to events during the year and many of your meetings will be in response to this cycle. See photocopiable pages 59–61 for an example of termly tasks.

- Teaching and Learning Responsibility (TLR) points offer a school the opportunity to create project leaders rather than subject leaders. Increasingly schools require teachers to lead aspects of education, such as international links or sustainability, rather than subjects.

You Can... **Work with stakeholders**

You Can... Empower middle leaders

Middle leaders are often the nuts and bolts of organisations. They are the flag bearers for their responsibility (often subject-based but increasingly this is becoming project- or theme-based). They are organisers and team managers. Particularly within primary schools, where we are required to be a 'Jack of all trades', subject knowledge can be perceived to play a key part within middle leadership. It is not uncommon for middle leaders to feel insecure if they believe that their subject knowledge is insufficient. It is the role of the senior leader to empower their colleagues and coach them towards being a leader from the middle.

Thinking points

- Middle leaders play a key role in implementing and embedding change within your establishment. To do this effectively they require the appropriate skills base that, in the past, may have been seen as part of the responsibility of the School Leadership Team (SLT). We have progressed a long way in our understanding of what leadership is and where it starts in school. Although there are varying subtleties a middle leader will, in many ways, require the same skills set as senior colleagues.

- There are a growing number of middle leadership courses and books becoming available (*You Can... Be an Effective Subject Leader*, © Scholastic, 2009, is the complementary book to this one for middle leadership). Middle leadership is not about how well you know your subject but about how well you lead it. Presenting that message to your middle leaders can circumnavigate insecurities about subject knowledge.

Tips, ideas and activities

- When a colleague takes up a new post, what mentoring systems do you have in place to ensure that they are successful? An experienced leader (either middle or senior) paired with a new leader can offer invaluable support.

- Changing colleagues' beliefs towards middle leadership can take time and you should prepare yourself for this while keeping in mind the type of leader you are trying to mould.

- Observation is often an area of concern. If this is the case then partner middle leaders with experienced teachers for paired observation. This provides an opportunity for quality assurance and adds professional weight to the process.

- Be prepared to listen. If you are coaching a middle leader (see page 10) then consider an 80/20 ratio to your talk time. They will, in all likelihood, know the answers to many of their queries and time for reflection will allow them to become autonomous leaders rather than dependent leaders.

- The National College for School Leadership (NCSL) offers a good programme for middle leadership (Leading from the Middle) that not only challenges middle leaders but also equips senior leaders with useful coaching skills. The programme covers five areas:
    - Leadership of innovation and change.
    - Knowledge and understanding of their role in leading teaching and learning.
    - Enhancing self-confidence and skills as team leaders.
    - Building team capacity through the efficient use of staff and resources.
    - Active engagement in self-directed change in a blended learning environment.

- The NCSL website, www.ncsl.org.uk, contains useful information that may support you and your middle leaders.

You Can... **Work with stakeholders**

You Can... Develop teaching assistants

Since 2000, a virtual army of adults has entered schools as teaching assistants. These roles range widely in style and need from working with individuals, to groups or whole classes as in the case of Higher Level Teaching Assistants (HLTAs). What has also grown is their profile with accredited courses, such as 'Helping in Schools', giving adults, in many cases parents, a way into the classroom that is meaningful and properly equips them for the learning world.

Thinking points

- *Developing people to support learning* (© TDA, 2006) was a strategy set out by the Teacher Development Agency (TDA) and School Workforce Development Board to:
   - Support schools as they develop new ways of training and deploying their support staff.
   - Create a framework of standards and qualifications to enable schools to develop the potential of all support staff.
   - Extend training opportunities to meet the development needs of all support staff.

This is in response to the need for a standard set of qualifications and skills needed by modern teaching assistants.

- You may be considering using teaching assistants or HLTAs to lead subject areas. With smaller schools there may be little choice and if your skills audit has identified potential, there is little reason not to utilise it. With teaching assistants you must, however, carefully consider their new responsibilities so that an accurate adjustment to their salary can be made (this is generally done by your local authority personnel department).

Tips, ideas and activities

- Performance management is an entitlement for all. If your school does not currently offer performance management, it would be worth visiting a local school that does to find out more.

- Who line manages this team? It may be appropriate for the SENCO to line manage them or another senior leader.

- How involved are your teaching assistants with school leadership? There is no reason why they cannot shadow subject or project leaders and act as a support for them.

- Skilled teaching assistants may well be the flag bearers you are looking for to lead a subject. For example, some schools use teaching assistants to model French or other languages during modern foreign language lessons because it is a particular strength of those individuals.

- Do your teaching assistants have appropriate child safety training? In many cases they are working more closely with individual children than teachers and appropriate safeguarding will help protect them and the children they work with.

- Teaching assistants are often meal supervisors. Having a split job dramatically changes their pay scales. If you are looking at retaining a good teaching assistant, changing their job description to full-time teaching assistant with lunchtime responsibilities will significantly increase their salary.

- Where appropriate, send your teaching assistants on the same courses as their partner teacher so that there is a shared understanding and accountability to follow through with the training in class.

- Below are some of useful websites that may support you and your teaching assistants:
   - www.classroom-assistant.net
   - www.teachernet.gov.uk (search for 'Teaching assistants').

You Can... **Work with stakeholders**

You Can... Give your children a voice

It is somewhat surprising that in the UK, children have had little input on the service that is provided for them. This is not the case with other western countries where, particularly in America and Canada, children have a long history of voicing opinions. This is slowly changing and is reflected within areas where the old style 'Education Service' has been rebranded as 'Children's Services'. There has also been considerable consultation with children as part of the Primary Curriculum for Change. With the renewed Primary Framework in place, the time is right to capitalise on what children have to say.

Thinking points

- What do we mean by the 'children's voice'? Certainly giving children a forum is important but allowing children access to the school and its mechanics demonstrates a conscious decision to involve them and value their views. This requires planning and will, if you have one, involve the school council. If children feel part of the process then they are far more likely to buy into it than if it is simply imposed upon them.

- If you are redesigning the curriculum, as many schools are at present, ask the children what they want to learn. It may be a golden opportunity to enable a child, who may not have been accessing the curriculum previously, to blossom in a subject they enjoy.

Tips, ideas and activities

- Most schools in the country run a school council. If this is new to you then School Councils UK (SCUK) offers good advice on the set-up process needed for an effective council. Equally, SCUK provides ideas on how to embed an established team. In many ways, they should be managed as you would any team within the school with a guiding set of principles, clear agenda and identified communications structure.

- Children will naturally want to help in school. Creating a structure of class helpers (or 'special agents' as one school calls them) who have clear responsibilities will seed the culture of structured and planned pupil support.

- Many American schools run 'buddy' schemes where older children (typically Year 5 or 6) act as friends during break times to younger children (typically Foundation Stage or Key Stage1). In order to become a buddy, a child will have to apply and be interviewed. This is best carried out by a senior member of staff to give it the appropriate sense of importance. Successful applicants (usually all of them) make up their own teams. Weekly meetings will offer the teams the opportunity to share things that have gone well or to be given some short professional development (such as learning a new game or how to react in conflict situations).

- Surveying children is a complicated task. Older year groups should be able to access most questionnaires and you may even want to consider creating online questionnaires (www.surveymonkey.com). However, younger children will need adapted versions. The key is to ensure that the same objective is being met by different versions of the questions.

- Below are a number of useful websites:
  - www.schoolcouncils.org
  - www.ncsl.org.uk (search for *Children's voices* and select the full report).

You Can... **Work with stakeholders**

You Can... Offer extended services at your school

Extended schools were born out of the Every Child Matters *agenda and a growing awareness of parental need. In 2008 one in three schools met the extended schools criteria and by 2010 all schools must offer or direct parents towards extended services and there is significant funding from the Government to ensure that this happens. For schools, in real terms, it means a thorough review of their site and opening times. Extended schools are required to be open 48 weeks a year from 8am–6pm. It is a dramatic change but a necessary one if schools are to meet the needs of their communities.*

Thinking points

- You are not going to able to offer every service for each defined 'reach group'. A reach group is a defined sector of the community you are aiming to support such as teenage parents, single parents, ethnic groups or fathers. Knowing that, consider what needs to be put into place to meet the needs of these groups and how your local networks communicate with each other.

- Increasingly, schools are being required to measure the impact of their extended schools activities on standards within the school. This is not necessarily an easy task as a significant element of after-school activities centre on enjoyment. That said, classes such as after-school booster clubs may well be established to meet the needs of specific children.

- By opening your school for longer hours you will, unfortunately, be more exposed to security breaches. Items such as data projectors, laptops and mobiles are highly desirable and they are easy to remove. Are your systems robust enough to minimise the risk?

Tips, ideas and activities

- What is the school community's need for extended provision? Increasingly, children come to school where there is no stay-at-home parent and where the role of a breakfast club meets their need.

- Breakfast clubs can access start-up grants from your local authority's business support officer. Consider the rise in food costs when writing a bid. Also highlight to your parent body that the provision is for early morning child care as well as a breakfast.

- What financial resources do you have to support low-income families?

- When establishing a new club, consider how to sell it. It may well be that a hook, such as a bespoke cap or T-shirt, may be enough to give it its own flavour (a good example is Computer Clubs for Girls: CC4G).

- There is evidence to suggest that extended services help to:
  - Improve pupil attainment, self-confidence, motivation and attendance.
  - Reduce exclusion rates.
  - Better enable teachers to focus on teaching and learning.
  - Enhance children's and families' access to services.

- Below are some of useful websites with information about extended schools:
  - www.cc4g.net
  - www.teachernet.gov.uk/wholeschool/extendedschools

You Can... Work with children's centres

The vision of children's centres is that they will be the hub of the community. By 2011 there will be over 3500 children's centres across the country giving all families and schools access to their services. Each centre will reflect the needs of its own particular ward. Children's centres have been introduced into communities since 2006 in three phases. Increasingly, phase three centres are linked to primary schools. For the first time, families will be able to access professionals from education, social services and health in one location for them to be part of their child's learning from birth.

Thinking points

- School-based children's centres offer professional development opportunities for school leaders, particularly talented deputy or assistant headteachers. In these cases it is an opportunity for them to lead a significant team, manage a sizable budget but also have the direct support of a headteacher as a mentor.

- Increased revenue budgets, particularly for site management, will enable schools to meet the 2010 requirement for the extended day (see page 37).

- Children's centres offer a rich resource for academic research. For the first time, long-term research on the impact of children's learning can take place in one location. Equally, models of staff structure and communication between agencies can be studied in order to identify good practice.

Tips, ideas and activities

- How does, or will, your school liaise with its local children's centre? There will be a range of services offered by your local centre that reflect the needs of the community. In many cases these will reflect needs within your school.

- Each children's centre will have a family support worker attached to it. These professionals can be invaluable in helping to support hard-to-reach groups and families.

- A significant aspect for ongoing consultation will be your Local Area Group (LAG). This will be made up of a range of interested parties including parents, teachers, health representatives, family support worker, service providers and professional carers. It is their role to monitor and evaluate the services provided by the children's centre.

- Through children's centres the Government has a commitment to offer:
    - The best start in life for every child.
    - Better opportunities for parents.
    - Affordable, good quality childcare.
    - Stronger and safer communities.

Your local children's centre will be working towards meeting these aims by supplying a Core Offer which includes:
- Early education integrated with full day care.
- Early identification of and provision for children with special educational needs.
- Parental outreach.
- Family support, including support for parents with special needs.
- Health services.
- Effective links with Jobcentre Plus.
- Local training providers: further and higher education institutions.

You Can... **Work with stakeholders**

You Can... Communicate with parents

Getting the communication between the school and parents right dramatically improves a child's opportunities to learn. When relations are clear and understood, parents will feel comfortable sending their child to school ready to learn. On the first day of school it is arguable that parents are more anxious than most children. Getting it right from the start can help smooth anxiety, which in turn provides a healthy platform of partnership between the school and the family.

Thinking points
- The way parents interact with schools is subtly different to a generation ago. Learning volunteers now have a higher profile, with a growing number of parents involving themselves in courses such as Helping in Schools where an accreditation can lead towards teaching assistant status. Not only does this encourage parental learning but it also exposes them to the day-to-day mechanics of a busy school, which are not always fully appreciated.

- Given the modern mobility of families it will not be uncommon to have parents within your community who have little or no understanding of the English language. What strategies do you have in place to ensure parental inclusion? Are your core documents and letters available in other languages? Do you buy into a translation service for consultation sessions? Naturally this will depend on the demands of your parents but parents have a right to clearly understand their child's academic progress.

Tips, ideas and activities
- What opportunities do parents have to get a flavour of the school before they even cross the threshold? Do you have a website that is up to date with clear images of what is going on in school? Do you have a presentational DVD? What does your prospectus look like? If you do not have the skills to produce high-quality media then there may well be someone on the staff or within the parenting community who can help. Top quality media gives a good impression of the school even before a new family has entered it.

- How active are your parent governors? They are your link with the parenting community and can lead on surveys, consultation and direct parents' views to the school. If you are developing a school vision then a parent governor is a vital member to involve as a voice for the families.

- What opportunities are there for parents to meet with staff? There are seasonal opportunities such as the autumn 'meet the teacher' evening and parent consultation nights throughout the year but you may want to consider options such as 'open classroom' days so that parents can get a feel of what the environment is like when their children are at work.

- How do you publicise your newsletters? Although they may well be given to each child, can you guarantee that parents actually receive it? Posting an enlarged copy on the parents' noticeboard will highlight that there is a new letter. Are you able to email a copy to parents directly? There are a growing number of services that will support the sending of bulk emails.

- There is no better way of communicating with parents than getting out into the playground at the start and end of the day. Any number of issues can be dealt with by teachers and yourself during these times.

You Can... **Work with stakeholders**

You Can... Report to school governors

There are few organisations that are directed by unpaid leaders such as the school governance system. However, an informed governing body can form the backbone of school improvement and be the energy that enthuses the parent body's support. The dynamics of a well-run School Leadership Team (SLT), supported by a knowledgeable governing body, can be impressive and are central to an effective school.

Thinking points

- Governors have three key tasks:
  - To provide strategic vision by setting the school's aims, polices and targets.
  - To act as a critical friend and challenging where appropriate.
  - To be accountable, including raising standards and managing the school's budget.

All of these tasks are undertaken in partnership with the school and the advice its leadership provides. Clear communication enables smart decisions.

- A key area for development for today's governors is succession planning. A significant percentage of current headteachers are nearing retirement with few looking to replace them. Planning for a smooth succession can take as long as nine months and should involve the whole school. It is something that all governors should be considering even if you or your headteacher is not within this bracket, as there is the genuine chance that other members of your leadership team will be stepping up to this role leaving potential skill gaps.

Tips, ideas and activities

- Know your audience. Governors are not, ordinarily, trained educators. Explain acronyms when they are used and try not to bulldoze your way through a report in an attempt to look like you know what you are talking about. They are there to support and can only do so when they have a clear understanding of what you are telling them.

- When you are called to report to the governors, ensure you provide the information they are looking for. An opening paragraph explaining the rationale will set the scene which in turn will help the governors to understand the report you have submitted. If a set of reports, such as end-of-year subject leaders' reports, are requested ensure the use of a common report framework with writer's guidelines. This continuity will support governors' understanding of the school's work.

- In order to continue to raise or maintain standards, schools need to evaluate core groups such as gender or ethnicity. It is the governors' duty to ensure that this happens. You should be prepared for some difficult questioning.

- Over 3000 schools are in the process of becoming children's centres. It is an opportunity to evaluate and streamline meetings to avoid duplication and wasted time. If you believe this is an area for development it would be wise to use a governor training session as a structured forum for debate.

- The governors and school leadership are a partnership. At least once a year arrange a light 'social' to enhance relationships.

- Agree times for meetings. It is not always possible for governors to meet during the day and both parties should be flexible for each other's needs.

- Below are a number of useful websites for governors:
  - www.governornet.co.uk
  - www.parentscentre.gov.uk
  - www.teachernet.gov.uk

You Can... **Work with stakeholders**

You Can... Develop international links

Perhaps more than before schools are sensitive to international events such as the Burmese cyclone, Chinese earthquake and the floods of 2007. These were unprecedented natural events that were at the end of a growing list of climate-related disasters. The Primary Review highlighted in its soundings (October 2007) the acute awareness that today's children have of the international community and the impact humans have on this planet. This is, in part, due to accelerated news brought on through the communications revolution, such as the internet. Now, more than ever, is a time for the learning lens to look outwards as well as inwards.

Thinking points

- The Primary Review, on its website's homepage, poses an interesting thought: 'The education children receive during their primary years is crucial for both their personal development and the country as a whole. But times are changing fast. We know that we must ask whether today's education is fit for tomorrow's world. We might also ask, no less insistently, whether tomorrow's world will be fit for today's children.' It could be argued that it is not enough to equip children academically. They must also understand their part as stewards of this planet.

- Communicating with other countries is as easy today as popping next door to a colleague's room. Social networking sites such as MySpace® and Facebook™ have broken international barriers. When international relations have been established, a webcam and Skype™ address are excellent for keeping the relationship active.

Tips, ideas and activities

- A school can sign up to varying levels of international commitment depending on the resources they have available (both financial and human). Often there are healthy funds that support projects with other countries and the experience gained from them far outweighs any financial costs. Below are examples of established programmes but it is highly likely that one of your local authority officers will have knowledge of other programmes that might fit the needs of your school.

- The National College for School Leadership (NCSL) currently runs an International Leadership Learning Programme (ILLP), which allows experienced school leaders an opportunity to reflect on their current practice within an international setting. Its core aims are to:
  - Enable participants to develop their own leadership capacity and that of others.
  - Ensure participants' schools benefit from knowledge and understanding of leadership practice overseas.
  - Enable the wider education system to benefit from learning on school leadership through a dedicated dissemination and knowledge management strategy.

- Comenius is part of the Lifelong Learning Programme (LLP) and provides opportunities for schools to introduce or improve the European dimension within their curriculum.

- The DCSF's Teachers' International Professional Development (TIPD) programme offers teachers the opportunity to visit other countries to get a taste of international education and the best practices used abroad.

- The League for Exchange of Commonwealth Teachers (LECT) creates links between teachers and educational leaders across the Commonwealth. It aims to promote excellence in education through using the international stage.

www.scholastic.co.uk   You Can... **Be a successful school leader 4–11**

You Can... Manage resources

You Can... Manage and develop your site

A site, like a home, is a responsibility. It is your responsibility to ensure that it provides a quality learning environment and it is the governors' responsibility to ensure that it is managed and in good physical condition. To this end, as with a home, you will need long-term investment and planning. The school's three-year budget should form the foundation for any development plans for the future. Your site reflects your educational ethos. It is your opportunity to make your mark and enhance children's long-term learning experience.

Thinking points

- For quite some time, secondary schools have viewed their site as a financial resource to be utilised. Primary schools have been slower in realising this potential market. However, there are many creative ways to utilise your school, for example, playgrounds can be let out to local clubs and equally, school halls can be made available for weekend hire providing much-needed space for children's parties. All of this goes towards the school budget and provides better resources for the children.

- Site management is essential for all lettings. Additional risk assessments will be required for markets or car parking. Some schools extend site managers' working weeks to cover these events but an alternative solution is to work with a third-party manager who shares the profits. Not only does this reduce the risk but also the administration for the school.

Tips, ideas and activities

- If your school is within a Network Learning Community (NLC – a cluster of primary and secondary schools that are local to your area) then skills and expertise can be shared across it. An NLC partner school may have already undergone a site review and could offer support and guidance.

- How old is your school? Recognising the age of the site will drive improvement plans particularly when they are linked to expensive improvements such as re-glazing or roof repair.

- Does your site meet new environmental specifications or educational needs? The Primary Strategy for Change is aiming to create a benchmark for all primaries to adhere to in much the same way as Building Schools for the Future is doing for secondary schools.

- How hard does your site work? Long gone are the days when schools were open from 9am–3.30pm but even fully extended sites can look at whether they are in the position to act as a market place over the weekend or car parking facility (particularly if your school falls near a large sports ground). There are creative opportunities for new funding streams and, if you are considering how to open your site beyond the core day, it would be useful to consult with a schools business advisor within your local authority.

- Below are some websites that may be of use:
  - www.ncsl.org.uk/programmes/bdp/sbmfuture/sbmfuture-sbd.cfm
  - www.haringey.gov.uk (search for *Consultation on the Primary Strategy for Change*).

You Can... **Manage ICT**

ICT has revolutionised almost every conceivable aspect of school life in recent years. While it continues to be true that there is nothing more powerful than a teacher leading their class's learning, the tools they use are unrecognisable from a decade ago, be it electronic tracking, digital tools such as the iPhone™ or the now-familiar interactive whiteboard. It is a brave new world that has sharpened the lens of learning.

Thinking points

- 'With every great device comes great responsibility.' It is a familiar type of saying but there is truth in it. We are all familiar with the potential abuses of the internet and how easily inappropriate material can filter through. If your school has not undergone rigorous e-safety training it should be considered as a matter of priority as the devices we use are becoming increasingly sophisticated and interconnected with the internet, making safety a high priority.

- ICT covers many areas of school but more humble devices such as cash tills used in the Foundation Stage or calculators are of equal importance. When evaluating your ICT capacity try not to overlook these familiar objects. If it is electric and delivers information, it is ICT.

Tips, ideas and activities

- The Government and schools have invested heavily in interactive whiteboards. So much so that publishing companies now consider the interactive whiteboard a given and produce resources reflecting this. As a school leader it is your responsibility to ensure that your colleagues are sufficiently trained to use these resources. Classrooms have changed and professional development must adapt. In all cases the interactive whiteboard is simply a tool. The teacher should use it to lead a lesson not the other way round. It is, however, an expensive tool and training should be sought – either internally or externally – to support colleagues.

- Organisation of your digital filing should reflect your physical files. For example, a subject leader may have folders that contain letters, budgets, action plans, audits and surveys. Digital folders should equally be organised so that a subject folder contains sub-folders with documents with similar titles. This will help when you are trying to find something on your computer as well as keeping your own personal systems clear.

- Increasingly, key documents have only been available online. The positive aspect of this is that documentation is available immediately and can be shared quickly. The negative aspect is that printing them can over time be costly, with the printed document having a shorter lifespan than a professionally produced one. As a result, printing should be carefully considered as it is not uncommon for a large percentage of the ICT budget to be dedicated to ink cartridge replacement, which could run into thousands of pounds.

- Below are a number of websites that may be of support:
    - www.dcsf.gov.uk
    - www.becta.org.uk
    - www.teachernet.gov.uk

You Can... Manage subject resources

The role of the subject leader is vital. They are the flag bearers who have the responsibility of enthusing and engaging your colleagues. Their leadership will direct a subject's course with the ultimate impact of raising children's standards. As a result they will be seen to be an expert and should be equipped accordingly. That said, within the primary sector we are often called to wear many hats and if you manage a subject area your skill will be to support colleagues by accurately directing them to appropriate experts, besides being expert in your own particular field of interest.

Thinking points

Subject leadership is changing in schools. It is not realistically possible for a colleague to remain a specific subject leader in an ever-evolving education climate. In response to this some schools are creating project leadership posts. These posts reflect key whole-school projects and are guided by the length of time that project is alive. For example, it may be an area linked to the school vision plan such as leading extended schools, or a DCSF initiative such as leading the implementation of the renewed Primary Framework. Not only does this allow subject leaders the freedom to move into new fields, it also moves the school's leadership structure away from subject specific leadership towards qualitative leadership. Although this requires a wholesale approach to all Teaching and Learning Responsibility points (TLRs), it will create a flexible leadership team in the long term.

Tips, ideas and activities

- How well do you know your subject? How well do your colleagues know your subject? Audits are useful to create a benchmark of skills and expertise. Your staff are your most expensive resource and should be equipped appropriately to meet their class's needs.

- How do you plan for your subject? The management of resources is a by-product of careful planning. If you have a budget, how it is used should be weighed against the needs of the school, which are driven by the vision and improvement plans.

- A school works in phases. Different aspects present themselves at different times of the year. See pages 59–61 for a timetable of benchmark events that should support your time management and help direct your action.

- Use your time wisely. Although all schools must provide PPA provision for all teachers during the working week, in reality this will only come to around two hours of non-contact time. It soon goes and schools are not required to provide additional time beyond this. Your personal time management supported by a robust action plan will help you to make the most of this time.

- Use other people's time wisely. Schools are busy places and good use of a diary can support other people's workload as much as your own. It is not reasonable to expect people to drop what they are doing in order to meet you ad hoc.

- The websites below may support your subject leadership:
  - www.standards.dfes.gov.uk/sie/si/SfCC/goodpractice/slmt
  - www.ncsl.org.uk (search for the PDF *The role and purpose of middle leaders in school*).

You Can... **Manage resources**

You Can... Manage a classroom

Being a school leader and class teacher is a challenge. However, at heart we all went into the profession to be teachers. Personal qualities for success may vary but a shared vision for learning coupled with enthusiasm and clarity of conduct are the same qualities needed for leadership. In truth we are all managers from the day we step into the classroom; the characteristics needed for managing a class are very similar to managing a school, it is merely the level of sophistication that changes.

Thinking points

- A senior school leader with a classroom responsibility has a challenging role. Unlike most headteachers, your role encompasses on-going planning, marking and assessment, which is a full-time job in itself. The NCSL research document *Leading from the Middle* made the recommendation of a minimum of 10 per cent non-contact time for assistant headteachers to undertake leadership tasks. This is not instead of PPA, which is to meet your teaching duties.

- Teaching assistant partnerships can blossom with school leaders. On a daily basis they experience your teaching style, which they will naturally mimic when teaching themselves. Equally, the teaching assistant can act as continuity when you are not in the classroom. Although controversial, your whole-school demands will, at times, supersede your classroom demands, which may result in periods of classroom absence. This can be cushioned by your teaching assistant's continued practice.

Tips, ideas and activities

- Organisation is key to a good lesson and will support your practice when you are called upon to launch from the classroom environment into the leadership one.

- Time manage yourself. If this is an area in which you feel you need support, talk to colleagues. If your subject area is new, there will be a learning curve which you should bear in mind.

- Be aware of your audience. If you are a lead teacher and you are being observed during a lesson, remember to take time to talk to the children about their performance while you are being observed so that they can have some feedback as well as you.

- Give your class your time. Children and parents value commitment and consistency.

- Use your class as a test base for new ideas. Children will sense your enthusiasm and can often offer good feedback if you are trialling a new resource or learning platform.

- Lists will help mark your success. It is very easy to get to the end of the day and feel that you have achieved little when the complete opposite may be true.

- Colleagues will look to you as an expert. Certainly if you're a subject leader it is wise to keep yourself abreast of changes and developments. Your subject expertise will primarily benefit your class but also go towards supporting colleagues around the school.

- There are plenty of websites and resources available on classroom management, for example:
    - http://drwilliampmartin.tripod.com/reallybest.htm
    - www.ncsl.org.uk (search for the PDF *Leading from the classroom*).

You Can... Manage risk

You Can... Assess risk

Risk assessment and safety are key areas of responsibility in the school. It is the headteacher's duty to ensure that appropriate personnel are placed to cover and monitor all potential areas of risk, and where risk is identified that appropriate action is developed thereby managing the risk and reducing its potential impact. Equally, it is every staff member's duty to act on areas of potential risk by having the skills to identify where these risks might occur and who to approach.

Thinking points

- In health and safety terms a 'hazard' is any situation that could cause harm such as a slippery floor or an unsafe act such as 'horseplay' or locations around the site that are of potential danger such as unofficial short cuts. Within this 'risk' is the potential it poses to an individual. It is, therefore, the establishment's responsibility to identify that risk and manage it.

- Children with particular needs, such as wheelchairs, will present new potential hazards that require risk assessments. Your local authority should be able to provide advice and support as well as the parents or previous school (if applicable).

- A failure to manage risk can not only have human and financial impact but can also damage the reputation of the school. A good reputation is important when attracting families and staff as it reflects good management.

Tips, ideas and activities

- Create a cross-party Health and Safety Committee that meets at least once every half term. The committee members should include the child protection officer, educational visits coordinator, a fire marshal, health officer (usually your primary first-aider), site manager and the headteacher who has overall responsibility.

- Ensure your educational visits coordinator is up to date with current practice. It could be argued that it is a child's right to be taken on educational visits but equally it is the teacher's responsibility to ensure that any appropriate risk-assessment forms and adult checks have been completed in good time before the visit.

- Each class must have a clear set of fire evacuation procedures. These should be practised at least every half-term with the fire marshal noting the time of day and length of time taken for the practice. Change the times of day that these practices occur as fires can happen at any time. It is advisable to have a secondary place for evacuation as a fire may be too close to your primary evacuation point.

- Plan for regular site walks with your site manager. You should be looking for areas of risk, some of which can be seasonal (for example, ice on the playground in winter, leaves in the gutter in autumn and nettles in the hedge during summer). Site walks should happen at least once every half-term. It is not possible to plan for every eventuality. If an extraordinary event occurs (such as flooding) you must evaluate the risk there and then and act promptly to minimise its impact.

- The website below may help when you are reviewing your risk-assessment procedures:
  - www.teachingexpertise.com (search for 'Conducting school risk assessment...').

You Can... **Manage risk**

You Can... **Recruit**

Teaching staff recruitment has a natural cycle, with the majority of recruitment falling between March and May. For other members of staff, such as administrators, site managers, meal supervisors, teaching assistants and even headteachers, this cycle does not generally apply. Recruitment carries a high risk as your candidates, if successful, will go on to represent your school. From your recruitment process you will want to know that your candidate is not only right for the school but will ensure the ongoing safeguarding of your pupils.

Thinking points

- Have you planned strategically and financially for recruitment during the coming year? Knowing your staff will allow you to anticipate where you may need maternity cover or where you suspect a member of staff may be leaving the school. An advertisement in a national paper can easily cost over £1000 and, if it has not been planned for, it can tip a school into a deficit budget.

- Safeguarding procedures should be set within your recruitment procedures to ensure that the person you recruit will reflect the safe environment of your school. That said, the Bichard Inquiry Report (2004, p12) stated that '[T]he harsh reality is that if a sufficiently devious person is determined to seek out opportunities to work their evil, no one can guarantee they will be stopped. Our task is to make it as difficult as possible for them to succeed...'. We must be vigilant.

Tips, ideas and activities

- Is your recruitment team trained? Do they understand the role they are going to play? A site manager's recruitment is very different to a headteacher's.

- Have you clearly defined the job specification and description? Have you specified in your advertisement that as a school you are committed to safeguarding?

- Are you clear about what type of interview you are going to conduct? A candidate may well be required to teach, so classes will need to be arranged.

- The standard procedure for recruitment is:
  1. Advertise the post including personal specifications.
  2. Send out information packs.
  3. Shortlist candidates for interview (this should be done by a minimum of two people).
  4. Obtain references (unless the candidate has requested they be obtained after the interview). General references should not be accepted alone. Even if the applicant has come from overseas, with modern technology it is relatively straightforward to obtain a current reference.
  5. Invite candidates to the interview.
  6. Conduct interviews and then 'score' the candidates.
  7. Make a conditional offer of employment pending all checks.

- Keep all records of the interview for six months should a candidate challenge your procedures and decisions.

- Be sensitive when giving feedback.

- If you do not believe that any candidates have met your requirements do not appoint. Although the interview procedure is expensive it is by far the cheaper option when securing the right person.

You Can... Manage risk

You Can... Undertake safeguarding measures

The Bichard Inquiry (set up as a result of the deaths of Jessica Chapman and Holly Wells in Soham in 2002) was commissioned to look at the ways employers recruit people to work with children and vulnerable adults. It highlighted the need for establishments, particularly schools, to undertake appropriate safeguarding measures to minimise the potential of unsuitable people working with these groups. Safeguarding, since then, has evolved into an element of Health and Safety to include school visits, recruitment and e-safety. There is little doubt that safeguarding, particularly within the digital world, will be an ongoing issue of great consideration.

Thinking points
- Within schools there are two keys points of contact where safeguarding can be addressed and potential incidents minimised:
    1. Through the interview process, which should deter 'risk' adults from applying.
    2. Through reasonable e-safety procedures.

- E-safety has evolved, among other things, as a result of cyber-bullying, online grooming and the ease of access to inappropriate material. E-safety is also an example of where safeguarding applies to colleagues as well as to the children they serve. Inevitably schools will become more connected to the digital world, particularly if technology continues to advance as rapidly as it is currently. Schools should consider what policy action they will take when using the internet and the reasonable steps to achieve this. We are preparing children for tomorrow's world, which will be a digitally connected one. We must consider what preparation is required to meet the children's learning needs while challenging our own e-superstitions.

Tips, ideas and activities
- Safeguarding covers four principle themes: emotional, physical and sexual abuse, and neglect. Do your colleagues understand what safeguarding means? Brainstorm ideas to help identify what it isn't as well as what it is. Some staff may need appropriate training.

- Are your colleagues aware of who to contact if they are concerned about a child being abused? Do you have a line of communication between yourself, social services and other link organisations (possibly a children's centre through a family support worker)?

- The *Staying Safe Action Plan*, written in response to the Staying Safe consultation, is the first ever cross-government strategy for improving children and young people's safety (www.everychildmatters.gov.uk/stayingsafe). The action plan sets out three main areas that can be used as part of a series of safeguarding training sessions for staff and governors:
    1. Universal safeguarding, involving work to keep all children and young people safe and to create safe environments for them.
    2. Targeted safeguarding to reduce the risks of harm for vulnerable groups of children and young people.
    3. Responsive safeguarding, involving responding effectively when children are harmed.

- Websites that discuss safeguarding measures include:
    - http://publications.teachernet.gov.uk (search for the PDF *What to do if you're worried a child is being abused*).
    - www.everychildmatters.gov.uk (search for the PDF *Guidance on the duty to safeguard and promote the welfare of children*).

You Can... **Manage risk**

You Can... Perform appropriate checks

We need little reminding of the tragic events of Soham in 2002 and its repercussions. As a result, and as an attempt to minimise opportunities for abusive individuals entering the education system, new safeguarding measures have been introduced with greater emphasis on List 99, the Protection of Children Act (POCA) list and enhanced Criminal Records Bureau (CRB) checks. This is a bureaucratic exercise but one that will go towards providing as secure an environment as practical for the children you serve.

Thinking points

- A List 99 and CRB check are only as current as the day that person was checked. As of spring 2008 all schools are required to regularly review each member of staff (at least every three years). This would include peripatetic teachers, extended-school club providers, parent helpers, occasional adults and all school personnel.

- CRB checks currently (2008) cost £36 each. As a school you should have a rolling three-year programme of CRB reviews and, as such, you will need to budget accordingly.

- Who is responsible for collecting the relevant information needed for either List 99 or CRB checks? Due to the nature of schools it often falls to educational visits coordinators who are responsible for evaluating risk on educational visits, including adult supervision. Consider how you share this information and, importantly, has your educational visits coordinator received appropriate, recent training?

Tips, ideas and activities

- During the years that checks have been in place, lessons have been learned about how to administer this workload but ultimately it is the school's duty to ensure that all appropriate safeguarding measures have taken place. The natural time for this is during an interview process as it will form part of that cycle.

- The challenging time is when teachers are preparing for school trips or inviting parent helpers into class. For this you will need a rigorous and tight policy that supports yourself and the children you care for.

- Ensure that all colleagues are aware of the day-to-day practices of your criminal checking procedures. A good time of year to re-visit this is at the start of September.

- Is your central staff report record up to date? It should include the names of all permanent colleagues as well as the names of day-to-day supply teachers, governors and regular adults. As with CRB checks, you will have to consider who is responsible for collecting and storing these records within your organisation but as headteacher or school leader it is your responsibility to ensure that this is done and that you know who is on the report.

- Before 2010 a new authority, the Independent Safeguarding Authority (ISA), will be established. Adults working with or for children will be required to join this authority and it will be their responsibility, to ensure this happens.

- CRB checks are now no longer portable and must be conducted fresh with each new placement regardless of when the last check was taken.

- Below are some useful sites regarding criminal checks:
  - www.isa-gov.org.uk
  - http://publications.teachernet.gov.uk (search for the latest PDF *Safeguarding children and safer recruitment in education*).

www.scholastic.co.uk

You Can... **Be a successful school leader 4–11** **49**

You Can... Resolve complaints

All schools, in accordance with section 29 of the Education Act 2002, must have a complaints procedure to deal with complaints and concerns addressed to the school about the service it provides. The responsibility for maintaining and monitoring this lies with the governors but the reality is that, for the most part, concerns are first raised with class teachers who, accordingly, should be trained in how to address concerns professionally to minimise the number of complaints raised to the headteacher and beyond.

Thinking points

- Schools should be aware of what a 'complaint' is and what a 'concern' is. Concerns should be dealt with informally and as early as possible thereby reducing the number of concerns that become complaints. Equally, your complaints procedures should work towards supporting informal resolutions. In most cases this will be managed by the class teacher as they are usually the first individual that parents/carers would approach. In many cases, concerns can be dealt with on the spot which may include an apology from individuals.

- Not all complaints are appropriate for schools to resolve themselves. These include:
  - Complaints against the curriculum.
  - Admissions or transfers.
  - Appeals for SEN.
  - Grievance or disciplinary procedures.
  - Complaints about collective worship.

Tips, ideas and activities

- Deal with complaints promptly. This gives a sense that, as a leader, you are in control of the situation and are taking the complaint seriously.

- An effective complaints procedure should:
  - Encourage resolution by informal means wherever possible.
  - Be accessible and publicised (often in the school prospectus).
  - Be simple to understand.
  - Be impartial.
  - Have established time limits for action and communication.
  - Ensure the right person is investigating the situation.
  - Respect confidentiality.
  - Address the points raised, with the information passed to the school leadership team so they can improve the service.

- Third parties, such as children's centres and extended-school providers, should have their own complaints procedures to which schools can refer.

- If complaints are not resolved by the headteacher they will go to a board of between three and five governors. If this does not resolve the complaint it can go to the DCSF. In all cases, ensure you have clearly logged each step of the procedure, the action taken and the time taken for the action to ensure transparency.

- Learn from the experience. A complaint, although uncomfortable, reveals aspects of the establishment that need attention.

- Know what your local authority's procedures are. Each authority should be able to provide you with guidance on complaints procedures, which should be in line with the DCSF model.

You Can... **Manage risk**

You Can... Understand child protection

The child protection officer has an almost unique position within the school because they act as the central point of reference for a wide range of services. The events leading to the death of Victoria Climbié and the subsequent report by Lord Laming, Keeping Children Safe identified the need for different agencies to work together to ensure good practice across all groups and to learn lessons from this tragic event. It is a great part of the role of the child protection officer to ensure that communication is concise, timely and relevant.

Thinking points

- Each school should have 'a senior member of the school's management structure... designated to take lead responsibility for dealing with child protection issues and liaising with other agencies'.

- 'The designated person need not be a teacher but must have the status and authority within the school management structure to carry out the duties of the post... including committing resources to child protection matters, and where appropriate directing other staff.'

- 'In many independent schools a single designated person will be sufficient, but a deputy should be available to act in the designated person's absence, and in schools which are organised into separate junior and senior parts on different sites or with a sperate management line, there should be a designated person for each part or site.' (Extracts taken from *Safeguarding Children and Safer Recruitment in Education*, DfES, 2006.)

Tips, ideas and activities

- If you have gone more than two years without any significant child protection training, then you should consider a refresher course as a matter of urgency.

- How well trained are your staff? Although your teachers have the greatest contact with children, it may be a teaching assistant or meal supervisor who identifies a cause for concern. Do they know what procedures to follow?

- Do you have a child protection structure in place? Who deputises when the named person is unable to act as child protection officer?

- As a school, do you log all instances where reasonable restraint has been used to protect a child or others from harm? Do you record any injuries or accidents that have occurred in school in the accident log?

- Does child protection form a part of your health and safety committee?

- Where there is a disclosure are there clear procedures for record keeping? Any allegations of abuse must be dealt with immediately. Do you have the proper systems in place to ensure this if the senior member of staff is unavailable?

- Ultimately, the overarching principle of all child protection is the welfare of the child and therefore no information can be kept in confidence if there is any risk to the child. A teacher has a duty of care to all children and therefore should not make promises of trust to a child when it is against their well-being and compromises safeguarding policies.

- A full copy of Lord Laming's report, Keeping Children Safe, can be obtained from http://publications.teachernet.gov.uk

You Can... **Manage risk**

You Can... Implement a School Travel Plan

By 2009 all schools in England must have a School Travel Plan (STP). This is already current practice in Wales and Scotland. Your STP is an action plan aimed at promoting environmentally sustainable forms of travel to school. Your school will have an allocated local authority school travel adviser who will not only assist you in writing the STP but will also support you in collecting evidence for it from surveys and walkabouts in the local area. They will also advise you on how to apply for grants.

Thinking points

- The DCSF/DfT will give a grant to every English state school that implements a STP to help fund measures identified in the STP, such as cycle parking, lockers and bus bays. Details are available from local authority school travel advisers. To be eligible, the STP must meet minimum criteria; your school travel adviser can help with this.

- Consider how you can match travel initiatives with existing projects. For example, a school in North London began running early morning cycle training sessions as part of its breakfast club. Through a grant from the DCFS and an award from Breakfast Clubs UK it was able to purchase five bikes and train an adult to a national cycle training standard.

- Talk to your school council, parent/staff association, governors and teaching staff about how they believe the school could change its modes of travel. This will increase the support of any projects or activities that you may run during the period of the STP.

Tips, ideas and activities

- Contact your school travel adviser. They have access to a wide range of resources and grants that can support your STP.

- Since STPs were introduced in 2004 a wide range of events and projects have been launched – keep an eye out for them, particularly those connected to Sustrans (website below) who were awarded £50 million through the People's Lottery Grant in December 2007.

- Be bold with your plan. This is a golden opportunity to build that needed crossing, to officially reduce the speed on your school's road, to repave the pavement, to construct a cycle storage area or a shelter for the end-of-day pick-up. If you don't put it into your STP it can't be considered for the grant.

- The following list is a basic guide to what a School Travel Plan should contain:
    - A description of the location, size and type of school.
    - A brief description of the travel/transport problems faced by the school/cluster of schools.
    - Journeys to and from school.
    - The results of a survey to identify how children currently travel to/from school and how they would like to travel to/from school.
    - Clearly defined targets and objectives.
    - Details of proposed measures.
    - A detailed timetable for implementation.
    - Clearly defined responsibilities.
    - Evidence that all interested parties have been consulted.
    - Proposals for monitoring and review.

- Below are a number of useful websites that could help inform, resource and develop a School Travel Plan:
    - www.sustrans.co.uk
    - www.schooltravelplans.org
    - www.teachernet.gov.uk ('School travel adviser toolkit').

You Can... Get to grips with core documentation

You Can... Use books and documentation to support your leadership

Although 'leadership' is a relatively new term within education it has deep roots within society. Larger bookshops almost always have a leadership section where 'what makes a leader' will be explored in varying depths. Business, in particular, has carried out a great deal of research to find out what leadership means and can offer genuine advice to education. Increasingly, books such as this one reflect the need for bite-sized pieces of information. However, it is worth taking the time to read weightier books. Be realistic – leaders are busy people so set aside one book a year that you will read. It will be worth the work.

Tips, ideas and activities

- If you do not have the time to read a book, it is likely you will be able to obtain an audio version of it. Websites such as www.audible.com have a comprehensive list of titles.

- Michael Fullan's seminal book, *Leading in a Culture of Change* (Jossey-Bass, 2001), sets out what impact change can have on a school and what school leaders can do to manage this. The book is an introduction to the topic of change but is enough to provide some useful tools for day-to-day management. His style is light and the book can be read in one evening.

- Daniel P Goleman has had almost universal acclaim for his book *Emotional Intelligence* (Bloomsbury, 1996). Set within the boundaries of education and business it explores where conscious emotional intelligence can be of greater value than academic intelligence. It is also available as an audio book.

- Malcolm Gladwell is author of *The Tipping Point* (Abacus, 2001) and *Blink* (Penguin, 2006) both of which are explorations of how we think, what affects our decisions and how to capitalise on those decisions. His style is sharp and intelligent – a good summer read!

- In *The 7 Habits of Highly Effective People* (Simon and Schuster, 1990) Steven R Covey conveys in seven chapters a series of lessons about how to improve your self-worth. Originally listed as a self-help book it has been widely adopted by those within all walks of leadership.

Thinking points

- As a leader it is in your best interests to be current in your thinking. Briefing events will help but you will have a large of amount of reading to consume. Read with care and intelligence. Do not be afraid to skim but equally do not skim to the point where you have taken nothing in. It can be a tricky skill to develop but one that can be refined with time.

- Know where to access relevant information. Governor's briefing notes will indicate short-term action and the education department's website will contain all common documents. If a document is only available as a Portable Document Format (PDF), as is increasingly the case, you must be able to access and store it. If you do not know how to do this, find out.

You Can... **Get to grips with core documentation**

You Can... # Use the internet to support your leadership

The internet has changed a great deal in the ten or so years it has been in the public domain. Before the millennium we were satisfied with simple searches and had a shared excitement in the potential of this new communication device. Now that we are comfortable with what it offers, our demands are greater. As school leaders we must equip ourselves with all that the internet can offer, understanding what risks its poses but equally taking risks in order to improve communication at all levels.

Thinking points

- The way adults use the web is vastly different compared to the children we teach. Our demands are principally for information, be that as a search or for shopping. Children's use of the internet is far more comprehensive and involves sophisticated social networking models and multimedia. This is an extension of how the internet has evolved from the original model that Sir Tim Berners-Lee envisioned nearly twenty years ago.

- The evolution of the internet and how it is utilised is often referred to as Web 2.0, this is in keeping with technical references to product updates. Unlike a product update, the internet itself has not changed. It is not the case that there is a Web 1.0 and then a higher order Web 2.0, they are both one of the same. It is the service provision that has changed with streaming video content and mobile internet availability.

Tips, ideas and activities

- The National College for School Leadership (NCSL) has a vast library of resources available for leadership development. Three of its core programmes (Leading from the Middle, Leadership Pathways and NPQH) use the internet for professional development by creating a virtual school. It provides an online reflections journal, involves colleagues in diagnostic reports as well as providing the familiar written material that we usually associate with the internet.

- Both the DCFS and NCSL websites have Portable Document Format (PDF) – effectively an electronic book version of most of their documentation. This allows the user to download booklets regardless of publication availability. Given the sheer amount of literature it has the added bonus of the user being able to save it on their computer without risking loss or damage. Printing is a cost that should be considered.

- E-safety must be considered at all levels and the BECTA website (www.becta.org.uk) offers good advice that can be tailored to a school's needs.

- Increasingly administration tools are now available on the internet, a trend that is set to rise given the growing platforms through which the internet can be received. Although these early versions should be viewed with some caution there is little doubt that within the next five years online administration tools will offer greater flexibility of access.

- Tools such as the BlackBerry© or Apple's iPhone™ are enterprise devices. They are commonly used within business for shared calendars, email, internet access and so on before their function as a phone is considered. Schools are way behind in this aspect. There are far more productive things for members of the School Leadership Team to be doing than swapping diary information. Online diaries (such as Google™ Calendar) allow people to view each other's diaries.

You Can... **Get to grips with core documentation**

You Can... Ensure every child matters

In 2003, the Government published a green paper titled Every Child Matters (ECM) *in response to the findings of the death of Victoria Climbié. It addressed the need for services to work in closer partnership, detailing four core themes: increasing the focus on supporting families and carers; ensuring intervention takes place before children reach crisis point; addressing the key problems identified in the Victoria Climbié report; ensuring that the people working with children are valued, rewarded and trained. As a result of this report, the Children Act 2004 and subsequent* ECM *papers,* Every Child Matters *has caused a deep-seated change for all of the children's services.*

Thinking points
- The last few years have shown that, academically, we have reached a plateau. If standards are to continue rising then school leaders will need to take a broader view of children's needs. Effective school leaders will recognise the value of *ECM* and reinforce its message to their colleagues. The *ECM* agenda can support children to break through barriers to learning.

- The *ECM* agenda is enormous. No one school leader and no one school can manage it alone. It demands a renewed approach to leadership and demands a renewed lens on learning. Effective school leaders will need to harness their colleagues' strengths and, through creative use of Teaching and Learning Responsibility (TLR) points, restructure their school leadership so that it can begin to address the *ECM* outcomes with true meaning.

Tips, ideas and activities
- *ECM* is about many agencies working together in partnership with an agreed format. As a result, Common Assessment Formats (CAFs) have been developed that address all the requirements of the services involved with any particular child.

- There are five key *Every Child Matters* outcomes:
  - Be healthy.
  - Stay safe.
  - Enjoy and achieve.
  - Make a positive contribution.
  - Achieve economic well-being.

- Extended schools and children's centres are offering wider opportunities for schools to create new partnerships. These partnerships demonstrate willingness for the school to look beyond its own skills base while offering broader learning opportunities for their children and families.

- By its very nature, *ECM* is individualised and school leaders will need to embrace in-depth consultation at all levels of their school community.

- Professional development is a necessary aspect of *ECM* and school leaders will need to lead this, particularly when enhancing the range of emotional intelligences needed to work with a growing range of professionals.

- Visit the *Every Child Matters* website for further information: www.everychildmatters.gov.uk

You Can... **Get to grips with core documentation**

You Can... Implement the renewed Primary Framework

It has been ten years since maths (née numeracy) and literacy parted company from the National Curriculum to be presented to teachers as National Strategies. This was a unique undertaking and, although it has had its fair share of critics, teachers have been given access to an unprecedented quantity of resources and professional development that is still growing. The renewed Primary Framework has taken lessons from the old, with particular note for literacy, which has been slimmed down to twelve strands (maths has seven) and can be viewed over two A4 pages. Although their foundations still remain within the National Curriculum they are very much viewed as their own entities.

Thinking points

- Literacy and maths dominate the curriculum. In most schools fifty per cent of the day will be given over to these subjects. It goes without saying that this creates enormous pressure on the remaining areas. The first *Excellence and Enjoyment* document (DfES, 2003) gave schools licence to adjust the curriculum to meet the needs of their learners. Yet a surprisingly large number of schools are cautious about going down the 'creative road'. The question has to be why? Is there a sense that standards may be compromised within a highly tested environment or is it a fear of perceived woolly teaching?

- Schools are no longer just centres for academic excellence. Now there are community, social and health partnerships that compete for school time. This is a positive move in supporting families but as a senior school leader you will have less time to develop the frameworks compared to ten years ago and this will require creative management.

Tips, ideas and activities

- Ensure your framework leaders are current in their knowledge and that they are able to identify where professional development is required.

- The slimmed down framework now offers an opportunity for a creative curriculum. Without the dozens of learning objectives from the previous version, teachers should be able to quickly identify cross-curricular links. It is learning objectives that count and not the quantity of lessons. If a child has learned the objective they should move on.

- Out of the twelve strands for literacy, four have some form of Speaking and listening focus, a far higher percentage than in the previous document. Is this reflected in planning?

- The framework is not statutory – only the National Curriculum is. If you are using the framework you must have adopted the renewed versions by September 2009. During the lead-in period, ensure that training is tailored to your school and avoid the old-style 'scripts'.

- It is good practice that an area of school improvement will be an aspect of the framework, often identified through assessment procedures. Once identified inform your governors of the area for improvement and delegate any action plans that need to be developed.

- What is your leadership structure? Who has overall responsibility for the curriculum and do they delegate appropriately? If a framework leader is not represented on the School Leadership Team what are the communication channels?

You Can... **Get to grips with core documentation**

You Can... Begin to understand the primary curriculum review and the Primary Review

Although the National Curriculum had a small re-shuffle in 1999 it has not significantly changed since 1995. Much of its content is still relevant to today's children but what has changed is the amount teachers are being required to teach. Modern foreign languages, SEAL and more singing in class are just three proposals from 2006–2007. In January 2008 an independent review of the primary curriculum began. Coupled with the Primary Review, the second decade of this century looks to be a period of significant change within the primary sector.

Thinking points
- Schools are now familiar with changing 'goal posts' in learning criteria. The question is do you have the capacity to manage the change? Part of that management will be knowing what's around the corner and preparing yourself and your team for it. The primary curriculum review will commence its statutory consultation in April 2009 and begin the support for implementation in September 2010 with the expectation that schools will first begin teaching the new curriculum in September 2011.

- Bringing families and the community into the debate is seen as central to the Primary Review. It is another reflection of the growing change that schools face. No longer are they isolated institutions (and many would argue they have never been) but now schools need to address how they can reach into the community and how the community can reach into them.

Tips, ideas and activities
Primary curriculum review
- The primary curriculum review is focusing on five aspects. These aspects were distilled from Ed Balls' (MP) invitation to Sir Jim Rose to lead the review:
   - In relation to the curriculum, what is reasonable to expect schools to provide and manage within the statutory time requirements of the primary school day?
   - Should primary pupils continue to be introduced to all the subjects of the National Curriculum from Year 1?
   - What should be the position of science and ICT within the primary curriculum?
   - Should some of the Early Years Foundation Stage areas of learning and development and pedagogy be extended into the primary curriculum?
   - What is the case and scope of reducing prescription and content in the Programmes of Study?

- Knowing what the focus for the review will be is an opportunity to evaluate your current practice. Many schools operate some or all of the five aspects. Common sense says that if there are more suggested hours of subject content than the day can offer then not all of it will be taught.

Primary Review
- The Primary Review has many outcomes but in principle it is to stimulate debate about the current condition and achievements of state primary education in England, and its future purposes and character. It seeks to involve not just professionals and policy-makers but also parents, children and the wider public. It is a policy document for the future but the planning for it must be addressed today. Visit the Primary Review website: www.theprimaryreview.org.uk

You Can... **Get to grips with core documentation**

You Can... Apply for Kitemarks

Kitemarks are an acknowledgment of a standard being met. Some are harder to obtain than others but within a sector of education where the practitioners are generalists, a Kitemark can point towards a specific area of strength within the school. As of 2007 there is now a Kitemarks 'tick box' at the front of the school self-evaluation document where all the major marks are represented. This has increased the need for schools to apply for these marks as they also help inform an Ofsted inspection. No longer can schools be shrinking violets – if you are good at something then get it acknowledged!

Thinking points

- Applying for Kitemarks takes a considerable amount of time. The BECTA and Artsmark documents are particularly lengthy. With these particular marks it is reasonable to consider them a high enough priority to add them to your School Improvement Plan (SIP) objectives. This will send a clear message to the subject leader who will be undertaking the work that the school, including the governors, see this as a high priority and will justify any costs incurred for completing the necessary paperwork (this could include supply cover).

- Most Kitemarks have a lifespan of three years. If it is older than that then questions may asked by an inspection team (be it Ofsted or your School Improvement Partner) as to the relevance of the mark within the current school climate. As with subject or policy development you may want to consider keeping a log and subsequent rolling programme to monitor the mark's life span. All marks can be added to school headed paper and other appropriate forms of communication, such as the school's website.

Tips, ideas and activities

Below are a number of Kitemarks that schools can work towards that are recognised by Ofsted and HMI.

- **Eco-School Status** – this is an international award programme aimed at guiding schools along their 'sustainable journey'. It is the Government's aim that, by 2020, all schools will be sustainable. There are three award levels: Bronze, Silver and Green Flag. www.eco-schools.org.uk

- **BECTA ICT Mark** – this mark is a reflection of a school's mature use of ICT. It is a comprehensive review of all uses of ICT across the learning community. It will take one year to complete the process. www.becta.org.uk/schools ictmark

- **Healthy Schools** – the overall aim of this accreditation is for schools to become healthier places through supporting the development and improvement of health-related programmes. www.healthyschools.gov.uk

- **Investors in People (IIP)** – established in 1990, this mark was first created for businesses who wished to demonstrate their management of staff. Over 37,000 businesses and schools have since worked through the IIP process. It is now possible to complete the process, in part, through an online tool kit. www.investorsinpeople.co.uk

- **Artsmark** – this is a national award scheme managed by the Arts Council England that recognises a school's high level of provision. There are three levels of award (Bronze, Silver and Gold). It is a thorough process that realistically takes one year to complete. www.artscouncil.org.uk/artsmark

- **Leading Parent Partnership Award (LPPA)** – this is a framework to enable schools to strengthen their relationships with parents and carers. The award is taken over 18–24 months, during which time a school will collect evidence to support the ten LPPA objectives. www.lppa.co.uk

School self-review and SEF update calendar – autumn term

When	What	Who	Notes on action
September	Walkabouts to review classrooms in relation to whole-school agreements and policies.	School Leadership Team.	
October	Discuss local authority data analysis for literacy and maths (KS1 and KS2) and Foundation Stage profiles. Look at implications for school improvement.	School Leadership Team and Foundation Stage coordinator.	
November	Review standards (RAISEonline) and implications for action. UPDATE SEF SECTION 3: Achievement and standards.	School Leadership Team.	
November	Monitor planning in all year groups.	Headteacher (following School Leadership Team discussion).	
November	Set Y2 and Y6 targets for current Y1 and Y5 pupils.	All coordinators.	
November	Update and analyse pupil-tracking sheets. Identify groups for interventions.	Y1 and Y5 class teachers with School Leadership Team.	
November	Collect and analyse whole-school data.	Class teachers.	
		School Leadership Team and coordinators.	
December	Conduct a staff questionnaire during staff meeting time to evaluate views on literacy, maths, CPD, ethos and support and other aspects of school functioning.	School Leadership Team.	
December	Analysis to consider implications arising from staff questionnaire.	School Leadership Team.	

PHOTOCOPIABLE

School self-review and SEF update calendar – spring term

When	What	Who	Notes on action
January	UPDATE SEF SECTION 1: Characteristics of your school (following January PLASC).	Headteacher.	
January	Plan the CPD programme in line with identified school improvement priorities.	School Leadership Team.	
February	Subject scrutiny (typically a book scrutiny or similar task).	Subject coordinators and School Leadership Team.	
February	Mid-year subject leadership team meetings to review progress.	Subject coordinators.	
February	Conduct and analyse a pupil questionnaire.	School Leadership Team.	
February/March	UPDATE SEF SECTION 4: Personal development and well-being.	Headteacher and School Leadership Team.	
March	Governing body self-review.	Governing body.	
March	Identify budget needs based on the SIP, last year's budget and known needs.	Subject coordinators.	
March	Update and analyse pupil-tracking sheets and evaluate interventions.	All staff and School Leadership Team.	
March	Pupil conferencing and target sharing.	Teachers and pupils.	
March	Team leader and mentor leadership meeting: focus – budget setting.	Subject coordinator and School Leadership Team.	
March	Hold a 'focus week' to evaluate standards in foundation subjects.	Foundation subject coordinators and School Leadership Team.	
March	Review attendance targets.	Headteacher and education welfare officer.	

You Can... Be a successful school leader 4–11   www.scholastic.co.uk

School self-review and SEF update calendar – summer term

When	What	Who	Notes on action
April/May	Plan the CPD programme in line with identified school improvement priorities.	School Leadership Team.	
June	Update and analyse pupil-tracking sheets. Science and ICT NC levels recorded. Collection of data.	All teaching staff. Subject coordinators. School Leadership Team and coordinators.	
June	Pupil conferencing and target sharing.	All teaching staff.	
June	Review action plan from previous year and identify action/needs for the coming year.	Subject coordinators.	
June	Review progress in achieving school improvement priorities and identify priorities emerging for coming year.	All teaching staff and the governing body.	
July	Conduct parent/carer questionnaire.	Parent governors and School Leadership Team.	
July	Coordinators' action plans reviewed and updated in line with SIP.	Curriculum coordinators.	
July	UPDATE SEF SECTION 2: Views of learners, parents carers, other stakeholders; SECTION 5: The quality of provision; SECTION 6: Leadership and management; SECTION 7: Overall effectiveness...	Headteacher and School Leadership Team. Headteacher, School Leadership Team and the governing body.	
July	Plan the CPD programme in line with identified school improvement priorities. Identify training needs for the coming year.	Subject coordinators and School Leadership Team. All coordinators.	
July	Review attendance targets.	Headteacher and education welfare officer.	

PHOTOCOPIABLE

School Improvement Plan

School name:	Links to school aims/vision:	*Every Child Matters* outcomes: • Being healthy • Staying safe • Enjoying & achieving • Making a positive contribution • Achieving economic well-being
Subject leader:	Objectives:	Success outcomes:
Academic year:		

Actions required (steps to be taken)	Action by whom	Action by when	Funding	Monitoring – how and who	Notes on progress

You Can... Be a successful school leader 4–11

Index

A
after-school booster clubs p37
Artsmark p58
Assessing Pupils' Progress (APP) programme p32
attributes of leadership p5, 6

B
BECTA ICT Mark p58
behaviour management p16, 28
books p11, 12, 33, 34, 53
breakfast clubs p37, 52
buddy schemes p36
budgets p9, 17, 29, 38, 42, 43, 47
bursars p17

C
characteristics of leadership p5, 6
child protection p51
children's centres p5, 26, 38, 40
Children's Plan (DCSF, 2007) p5
classroom management p14, 45
coaching p10, 14, 34
communication p8, 39, 54
community links p5, 7, 14, 16, 37, 38, 57
complaints p30, 50
Continuing Professional Development p12, 29
Criminal Records Bureau (CRB) checks p49
curriculum development p25, 27, 36, 56, 57

D
delegation p7, 19, 21

E
e-safety p43, 48, 54
Eco-School Status p58
effective schools p14, 40
electronic tracking p9, 32
emotional intelligence p10, 11
Every Child Matters (DfES, 2004) p5, 27, 55
Excellence and Enjoyment (DfES, 2003) p25, 29, 56
extended schools p5, 26, 27, 37, 42, 55

F
financial planning p17
future planning p26

G
governing bodies p13, 22, 29, 32, 33, 40, 50

H
health and safety p46, 48, 51
Healthy Schools Kitemark p58
Helping in Schools course p35, 39

I
ICT management p25, 43
improvement p18, 22, 23
inclusion p9, 39
Independent Safeguarding Authority (ISA) p49
international links p27, 41
internet support p54
Investors in People (IIP) p58

K
Kitemarks p58

L
lead learners p8
leadership resources p11, 12, 33, 34, 53
leadership structures p6, 24, 44, 56
leadership training p12, 13, 16, 34, 41, 54
Leading from the Middle (LftM) p13, 45
Leading Parent Partnership Award (LPPA) p58
League for Exchange of Commonwealth Teachers (LECT) p41
learning environment p8, 25
List 99 checks p49
Local Area Groups (LAG) p38

M
media links p20
mentoring p10, 30, 34
middle leaders p6, 13, 34

N
National College for School Leadership (NCSL) p7, 10, 12, 34, 41, 54
National Professional Qualification for Headship (NPQH) p13, 16
National Standards for Headteachers (DfES, 2004) p5, 7
National Strategies p27, 56
needs assessments p9
Network Learning Communities (NLC) p16, 42

O
observed teaching p30, 31, 34, 45
Ofsted p19, 23, 24, 30, 32, 58
organisation p14, 43, 45

P
parent governors p39
parent/school communication p39
partnerships p5, 23, 26, 38, 40, 55, 56
performance management p31, 35
planning for the future p26
potential leaders p13
press links p20
primary curriculum review p57
Primary Framework p44, 56
Primary National Strategies p27, 56
Primary Review p41, 57
professional development p7, 8, 9, 12, 13, 14, 16, 29, 54, 55, 56
project leaders p26, 33, 44
projected budgets p17
publicity p20, 39

Q
qualities of leadership p5, 6

R
RAISEonline p9, 32
recruitment p16, 47
research opportunities p38
resources p11, 12, 33, 34, 53
responsibility to lead p7, 8
risk assessments p46
risk-taking p25
role definition p7, 8
rural schools p16

S
safeguarding procedures p47, 48, 49
safety p46, 48, 51
school councils p36
School Improvement Partners p23, 58
School Improvement Plans p9, 22, 27, 31, 58, 62
School Leadership Teams p5, 7, 11, 19, 24, 26, 33, 54
school self-review p19, 59, 60, 61
School Travel Plans p52
Schools Forum p7
SEAL (Social and Emotional Aspects of Learning) p28
security issues p37
Self-Evaluation Forms p19, 24, 32, 59, 60, 61
shadow-staff structures p12, 13
site management p9, 38, 42, 46
skills audits p35, 44
small schools p16
smart objectives p31
Social and Emotional Aspects of Learning (SEAL) p28
staff communication p18, 19
staff support p14, 29, 35
Staying Safe Action Plan p48
subject resource management p44
succession of staff p12, 13, 15, 40
SureStart (2005) p9

T
Teachers' International Professional Development (TIPD) programme p41
Teachers TV p12, 20
Teaching and Leadership Awards p13
Teaching and Learning Responsibility (TLR) p7, 26, 33, 44, 55
teaching assistants p31, 35, 39, 45
time management p26, 44, 45
Training and Development Agency for Schools (TDA) p7, 8
travel initiatives p52

U
urban schools p15

V
vision, whole-school p12, 18, 39
visit management p46, 48, 49
voice of the child p36

W
well-being of staff p11, 29

SCHOLASTIC

Also available in this series:

YOU CAN Be an Effective SUBJECT LEADER — Anthony David — FOR AGES 4-11
ISBN 978-1407-10195-8

YOU CAN Be a Successful SCHOOL LEADER — Anthony David — FOR AGES 4-11
ISBN 978-1407-10196-5

YOU CAN Motivate reluctant readers — Kate Ruttle — FOR AGES 4-7
ISBN 978-1407-10173-6

YOU CAN Motivate reluctant readers — Kate Ruttle — FOR AGES 7-11
ISBN 978-1407-10174-3

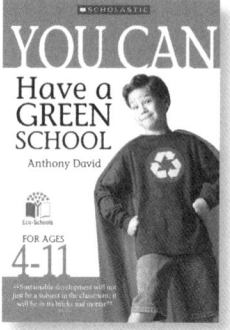

YOU CAN Have a GREEN SCHOOL — Anthony David — FOR AGES 4-11
ISBN 978-1407-10083-8

YOU CAN Make the most of the NATIONAL YEAR OF READING — Kate Ruttle — FOR AGES 4-7
ISBN 978-1407-10070-8

YOU CAN Have a CREATIVE classroom — Sue Cowley — FOR AGES 4-7
ISBN 978-0439-94534-9

YOU CAN Have a CREATIVE classroom — Sue Cowley — FOR AGES 7-11
ISBN 978-0439-94535-6

YOU CAN Create a CALM classroom — Sue Cowley — FOR AGES 4-7
ISBN 978-0439-96522-4

YOU CAN Create a CALM classroom — Sue Cowley — FOR AGES 7-11
ISBN 978-0439-96523-1

YOU CAN Survive your early years OFSTED inspection — Avril Harpley and Ann Roberts — FOR AGES 3-5
ISBN 978-0439-96534-7

YOU CAN Use an interactive WHITE BOARD — Julie Coyill — FOR AGES 4-7
ISBN 978-0439-96539-2

YOU CAN Use an interactive WHITE BOARD — Julie Coyill — FOR AGES 7-11
ISBN 978-0439-96540-8

YOU CAN Create a THINKING classroom — Sue Cowley — FOR AGES 4-7
ISBN 978-0439-96554-5

YOU CAN Create a THINKING classroom — Sue Cowley — FOR AGES 7-11
ISBN 978-0439-96555-2

YOU CAN Improve your children's WRITING — Celia Warren — FOR AGES 4-7
ISBN 978-0439-94530-1

YOU CAN Improve your children's WRITING — Celia Warren — FOR AGES 7-11
ISBN 978-0439-94531-8

YOU CAN Create an OUTDOOR classroom — FOR AGES 3-7
ISBN 978-0439-94559-2

YOU CAN Teach Phonics — FOR AGES 3-7
ISBN 978-0439-94554-7

YOU CAN Teach your class to LISTEN — Sue Palmer — FOR AGES 4-7
ISBN 978-0439-94532-5

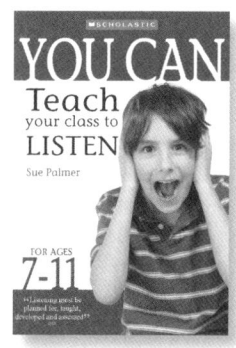

YOU CAN Teach your class to LISTEN — Sue Palmer — FOR AGES 7-11
ISBN 978-0439-94533-2

To find out more, call: 0845 603 9091
or visit our website www.scholastic.co.uk